The truth about socialism

Allan L. Benson

Alpha Editions

This edition published in 2024

ISBN : 9789362518651

Design and Setting By
Alpha Editions
www.alphaedis.com
Email - info@alphaedis.com

As per information held with us this book is in Public Domain.
This book is a reproduction of an important historical work. Alpha Editions uses the best technology to reproduce historical work in the same manner it was first published to preserve its original nature. Any marks or number seen are left intentionally to preserve its true form.

Contents

CHAPTER I TO THE DISINHERITED ....- 1 -
CHAPTER II WHAT SOCIALISM IS AND WHY IT IS ....- 3 -
CHAPTER III THE VIRTUOUS GRAFTERS AND THEIR GRAVE OBJECTIONS TO SOCIALISM ....- 15 -
CHAPTER IV WHY SOCIALISTS PREACH DISCONTENT ....- 27 -
CHAPTER V HOW THE PEOPLE MAY ACQUIRE THE TRUSTS...- 40 -
CHAPTER VI THE "PRIVATE PROPERTY " BOGEY-MAN ....- 51 -
CHAPTER VII SOCIALISM THE LONE FOE OF WAR.......- 62 -
CHAPTER VIII WHY SOCIALISTS OPPOSE "RADICAL" POLITICIANS ....- 76 -
CHAPTER IX THE TRUTH ABOUT THE COAL QUESTION..- 88 -
CHAPTER X DEATHBEDS AND DIVIDENDS ....- 97 -
CHAPTER XI IF NOT SOCIALISM—WHAT?...................- 106 -
APPENDIX. NATIONAL SOCIALIST PLATFORM ....- 117 -

CHAPTER I
TO THE DISINHERITED

I am going to put a new heart into you. I am going to put your shoulders back and your head up. Behind your tongue I shall put words, and behind your words I shall put power. Your dead hopes I shall drag back from the grave and make them live. Your live fears I shall put into the grave and make them die. I shall do all of these things and more by becoming your voice. I shall say what you have always thought, but did not say. And, when your own unspoken words come back to you, they will come back like rolling thunder.

This country belongs to the people who live in it.

The power that made the Rocky Mountains did not so make them that, viewed from aloft, they spell "Rockefeller."

The monogram of Morgan is nowhere worked out in the course of the Hudson River.

Nothing above ground or below ground indicates that this country was made for anybody in particular.

Everything above ground and below ground indicates that it was made for everybody.

Yet, this country, as it stands to-day, is not for everybody. Everybody has not an equal opportunity in it. A few do nothing and have everything. The rest do everything and have nothing.

A great many gentlemen are engaged in the occupation of trying to make these wrongs seem right. They write political platforms to make them seem right. They make political speeches to make them seem right. They go to Congress to make them seem right. Some go even to the White House to make them seem right. But no mere words, however fine, can make these wrongs right.

The conditions that exist in this country to-day are indefensible and intolerable. This should be a happy country. It should be a happy country because it contains an abundance of every element that is required to make happiness. The pangs of hunger should never come to a single human being, because we already produce as much food as we need, and with more intelligent effort could easily produce enough to supply a population ten times as great.

Yet, instead of this happy land, we have a land in which the task of making a living is constantly becoming greater and more uncertain. Everything seems to be tied up in a knot that is becoming tighter.

You do not know what is the matter.

Your neighbor does not know what is the matter.

Why should you know what is the matter?

You never listen to anybody who wants you to find out. You listen only to men who want to squeeze you out. Their word is good with you every time. You may not think it is good, but it is good. You may not take advice from Mr. Morgan, but you take advice from Mr. Morgan's Presidents, Congressmen, writers, and speakers. You may not take advice from Mr. Ryan, but you take advice from the men whom Mr. Ryan controls. If you should go straight to Mr. Ryan you would get the same advice. What these men say to you, Mr. Morgan and Mr. Ryan say to them. You listen as they speak. You vote as they vote. They get what they want. You don't get what you want. But you stick together. You seem never to grow tired. You were with them at the last election. Many of you will be with them at the next election. But you will not be with them for a while after the next election. They will go to their fine homes, while you go to your poor ones. They will take no fear with them, save the fear that some day you will wake up; that some day you will listen to men who talk to you as I am talking to you. But you will take the fear of poverty with you, and it will hang like a pall over your happiness.

If you have lost your hope of happiness, get it back. This can be a happy nation in your time. This country is for you. It is big. It is rich. It is all you need. But you will have to take it, and the easiest way to take it is with ballots.

CHAPTER II
WHAT SOCIALISM IS AND WHY IT IS

The occupation of the scarlet woman is said to be "the oldest profession." If so, the robbery of man by man is the oldest trade. It is as old as the human race. It had its origin in the difficulty of producing enough of the material necessities of life. The earth was lean. Man was weak. Never was there enough food for all. Many must suffer. Some must starve.

What wonder that man robbed man? Self-preservation is the first law of nature. We have always fought and shall always fight for those things that are scarce and without which we should die. If water were scarce, we should all be fighting by the brookside. If air were scarce, we should all be straining our lungs to take in as much as we could.

But what wonder, also, that the robbed should resist those who robbed them? The robbed, too, have the instinct of self-preservation. They, too, want to live. All through the ages, they have fought for the right to live. By the sheer force of numbers, they have driven their exploiters from pillar to post. Again and again, they have compelled their exploiters to abandon one method of robbery, only to see them take up another. And, though some men no longer own other men's bodies, some men still live by the sweat of other men's brows.

The question is: Must this go on forever? Must a few always live so far from poverty that they cannot see it, while the rest live so close to it that they cannot see anything else? Must millions of women work in factories at men's work, while millions of men walk the streets unable to get any work? Must the cry of child-labor forever sound to high heaven above the rumble of the mills that grind their bodies into dividends? Must the pinched faces of underfed children always make some places hideous?

No man in his senses will say that this situation must always exist. Human nature revolts at it. The wrong of it rouses the feelings even before it touches the intellect. Something within us tells us to cry out and to keep crying out until we find relief. We have tried almost every remedy that has been offered to us, but every remedy we have tried has failed. The hungry children are still with us. The hungry women are still with us. The hungry men are still with us. Never before was it so hard for most people to live. Yet, we live at a time when men, working with machinery, could make enough of everything for everybody.

Your radical Republican recognizes these facts and says something is the matter. Your Democratic radical recognizes these facts and says something is the matter. Your Rooseveltian Progressive also recognizes these facts and says something is the matter. But if you will carefully listen to these gentlemen, you will observe that none of them believes much is the matter. None of them believes much need be done to make everything right. One wants to loosen the tariff screw a little. The others want to put a new little wheel in the anti-trust machine.

Socialists differ from each of these gentlemen. Socialists say much is the matter with this country. Socialists say much is the matter with any country, most of whose people are in want or in fear of want, and some of whose people are where want never comes or can come. Some such conditions might have been tolerated a thousand years ago. Socialists will not tolerate them to-day. They say the time for poverty has passed. They say the time for poverty passed when man substituted steam and electricity for his muscles and machinery for his fingers.

But poverty did not go out when steam and electricity came in. On the contrary, the fear of want became intensified. Now, nobody who has not capital can live unless he can get a job. In the days that preceded the steam engine, nobody had to look for a job. Everybody owned his own job. The shoemaker could make shoes for his neighbors. The weaver could weave cloth. Each could work at his trade, without anybody's permission, because the tools of their trades were few and inexpensive. Now, neither of them can work at his trade, because the tools of his trade have become numerous and expensive. The tools of the shoemaker's trade are in the great factory that covers, perhaps, a dozen acres. The tools of the weaver's trade are in another enormous factory. Neither the shoemaker nor the weaver can ever hope to own the tools of his trade. Nor, with the little hand-tools of the past centuries, can either of them compete with the modern factories. The shoe trust, with steam, electricity and machinery, can make a pair of shoes at a price that no shoemaker, working by hand, could touch.

Thus the hand-workers have been driven to knock at the doors of the factories that rich men own and ask for work. If the rich men can see a profit in letting the poor men work, the poor men are permitted to work. If the rich men cannot see a profit in letting the poor men work, then the poor men may not work. Though there be the greatest need for shoes, if those in need have no money, the rich men lock up their factories and wave the workers away. The workers may starve, if they like. Their wives and children may starve. The workers may become tramps, criminals or maniacs; their wives and their little children may be driven into the street—but the rich men who closed their factories because they could see no profit in keeping them open—these rich men take no part of the responsibility. They talk about the "laws of trade," go to their clubs and have a little smoke, and, perhaps, the next week give a few dollars to "worthy charity" and forget all about the workers.

Now, the Socialists are extremely tired of all this. Their remedy may be all wrong, but they are tired of all this. Put the accent upon the *tired* all the time. They say it is all wrong. Not only do they say it is all wrong, but they say they know how to make it all right. They do not propose to do any small job of tinkering, because they say that if small jobs of tinkering were enough to cure the great evil of poverty, we should have cured it long ago. They say we have been tinkering with tariffs, income taxes and the money question for a hundred years without reducing either want or the fear of want. They say we have made no progress, during the last hundred years, in reducing want and the fear of want, because we have never hit the grafters where they live. By this, they mean that we have never cut the tap root upon which robbery grows. The serfs cut off the tap root when they threw off chattel slavery, but another tap root has grown and we have not yet discovered where to strike.

The Socialists say they know where to strike.

"*Strike at the machinery of the country,*" they say, "*by having the people, through the government, own the machinery of the country.*"

"*Cut out the profits of the private owners,*" they say. "*Let the people own the trusts and make things because they want the things, instead of because somebody else wants a profit, and there will never again be in this country either want or the fear of want.*"

This sounds like a nice, man-made program, cooked up late at night by some zealous gentleman intent upon saving his country. It may be a foolish program, but if it is, it is not that kind of a foolish program. It is not man-made, any more than Darwin's theory of evolution is man-made. Darwin observed present animal life and thereby explained the past. Socialists observe past and present industrial life and thereby forecast the future. Paradoxically, then, the Socialist remedy is not a Socialist remedy. If it is anything, it is the remedy that evolution is bringing to us. Socialists see what evolution is bringing and proclaim it, much as a trainman announces the coming of a train that he already sees rounding a curve.

Let me tell a story to illustrate this point:

Seventy years ago, Socialist writers predicted and accurately described the trusts as they exist to-day. Nobody paid much attention to the predictions or the descriptions. Nowhere in the world was there a single trust. Nowhere in the world was any one thinking of forming one. The first trust was not formed until almost forty years later.

The trusts were predicted because the steam engine had been invented and brought with it machinery. The invention did not mean much to most people. It meant everything to these early Socialists. They saw its significance. They saw that it meant a transformed world. Never again would the world be as it had always been. Never again would the amount of wealth that man could create be limited by his weak muscles. Steam and machinery had come to do, not only what he had been doing, but what he had never dreamed of doing.

The only lesson that the rich men of the day learned from steam was that it meant more money for them. The rich men of the day, by the way, were in need of a new method of exploitation. Serfdom had just gone down in the Napoleonic wars, and some men were no longer able to exploit other men by claiming to own the other men's bodies. Exploitation, through the private ownership of land, still continued, it is true, but a man working by hand cannot be much exploited because he cannot make much. What I mean by this is that he cannot be exploited of many dollars. Of course, he can be exploited of so great a percentage of his product that he is left starving, but the man who exploits him will not be much richer. That is why there were no great fortunes, as we now know them, in the days before the machinery age. Wealth was too difficult to make.

But, to return to our story. The invention of the steam engine gave the rich men of the early eighteenth century the opportunity of which they stood much in need. Factories cost money. The workers did not have any. The rich men did. The rich men built factories. That is to say, they thought they were only building factories. As a matter of fact, they were taking over, from the hands of evolution, the poor man's tools. Never again were working men to own the tools of their trades. Their tools had gone down in the struggle in which the survivors must be the fittest. For centuries, the world had starved because of their old hand-tools. They could not, for a moment, exist after steam and machinery came. It was right that the hand-tools should go. It was unfortunate for the workers only that the successors of hand-tools were too expensive for individual ownership, and that they were also unsuited to such ownership. No man can run a whole shoe factory, even if he owns one. Many men are required to run many machines, and many machines are required to make the labor of men most productive.

All of this, the early Socialists saw or reasoned out. They saw the rich men of the day building factories. They saw those who were not quite so rich joining together to build factories. Little co-partnerships were springing up all over the world. Everybody competed with everybody else in his line. Manufactures multiplied, and it became the common belief that "competition was the life of trade."

Stick a pin here. The roots of Socialism go down somewhere near this point.

The early Socialist writers who predicted the trusts did not believe competition was the life of trade. They believed the inevitable tendency of competition was to kill itself. Their reasoning took this form:

Manufacturers engage in business, not because they want to supply goods to the public, but because they want to make profits for themselves.

Inasmuch as the question of who shall make the profits depends upon who shall sell the goods, manufacturers will compete with each other to sell goods.

Manufacturers will be able to compete and still make a profit so long as the demand for goods far exceeds the supply.

But the demand for goods will not always far exceed the supply. The opportunity to make profits will tempt other capitalists to create manufacturing enterprises. The market will become glutted with goods, because more will have been produced than the people can pay for.

Competition among manufacturers will then become so fierce that profits will first shrink and eventually disappear.

Manufacturers, to regain their profits, will then cease to compete. The strongest will buy out or crush the weakest. Monopolies will be formed, primarily to end competition and save the competitors from themselves, but, having been formed, they will also be used to rob the people.

Mind you—this reasoning is not new. It is seventy years old. It sounds new only because it has so recently come true. Nobody whose eyes are open now believes that competition is the life of trade. The phrase has died upon the lips of the very men who used to speak it. The late Senator Hanna was one of the many who used to believe that good trade could not be where competition was not. But, when the great trust movement of 1898 was under way, Senator Hanna said: "It is not a question of whether business men do or do not believe in trusts. It is a question only of whether business men want to be killed by competition or saved by coöperation."

However, the existence of the trusts is ample verification of the Socialist prophecy that they would come. And the trusts came in the way that the early Socialists said they would come.

We may now proceed to consider what those early Socialist writers thought of the trusts that they so accurately described before they came, what they believed would become of them and what they believed would supplant them.

No Socialist was ever heard finding fault with a trust simply for existing. A Socialist would as soon find fault with a green apple because it had been produced from a blossom. In fact, Socialists regard the trusts as the green apples upon the tree of industrial evolution. But they would no more destroy these industrial green apples that are making the world sick than they would destroy the green apples that make small boys sick. They pause, first because they are evolutionists, not only in biology, but in everything; second, because they recall that the green apples that make the boy sick will, if left to ripen, make the man well. In short, Socialists regard trusts, or private monopolies, as a necessary stage in industrial evolution; a stage that we could not have avoided; a stage that in many respects, represents a great advance over any phase of civilization that preceded it, yet a stage at which we cannot stop unless civilization stops. Therefore, Socialists take this position:

It is flying in the face of evolution itself to talk about destroying, or even effectually regulating the trusts.

Private monopolies cannot be destroyed except as green apples can be destroyed—by crushing them and staying the evolutionary processes that, if left alone, will yield good fruit.

Private monopolies cannot be effectually regulated because, so long as they are permitted to exist, they will regulate the government instead of permitting the government to regulate them. They will regulate the government because the great profits at stake will give them the incentive to do so and the enormous capital at their command will give them the power to do so.

In other words, Socialists say that the processes of evolution should go on. What do they mean by this? They mean that the good elements of the trust principle should be preserved and the bad elements destroyed. What are the good elements? The economies of large, well-ordered production, and the avoidance of the waste due to haphazard, competitive production. And the bad elements? The powers that private monopoly gives, through control of market and governmental policies, to rob the consumer.

Socialists contend that the good can be saved and the bad destroyed by converting the private monopolies into public monopolies—in other words, by letting the government own the trusts and the people own the government. This may seem like what the foes of Socialism would call a "patent nostrum." It is nothing of the kind. It is no more a patent nostrum than the trusts are patent nostrums. Socialists invented neither private monopolies nor public monopolies. Socialists did not kill competition. Competition killed itself. Socialists simply were able to foresee that too much competition would end all competition and thus give birth to private monopoly.

And, having seen thus far, they looked a little further and saw that private monopoly would not be an unmixed blessing. They saw that under it, robbery would be practised in new, strange and colossal forms. They knew the people would not like robbery in any form. They knew they would cry out against it as they are crying out against the trusts to-day. And they believed that after having tried to destroy the trusts and failed at that; after having tried to regulate the trusts and failed at that, that the people would cease trying to buck evolution, and get for themselves the benefits of the trusts by owning them.

This may be an absurd idea, but in part, at least, it has already been verified. It has been demonstrated that private monopoly saves the enormous sums that were spent in the competitive era to determine whether this man or that man should get the profit upon the things you buy. The consumer has absolutely no interest in the identity of the capitalist who exploits him. But when capitalists were competing for trade, the consumer was made to bear the whole cost of fighting for his trade.

Private monopoly has largely done away with the cost of selling trust goods, by doing away with the individual competitors who were once struggling to put their goods upon the market. Private monopoly has also reduced the cost of production by introducing the innumerable economies that accompany large production.

What private monopoly has not done and will never do is to pass along these savings to the consumers. The monopolists have passed along some of the savings, but not many of them. What they have passed along bears but a small proportion to what they have kept. That is what most of the trouble is about now. The people find it increasingly difficult to live. For a dozen years, it has been increasingly difficult to live. Persistent and more persistent has been the demand that something be done about the trusts.

The first demand was that the trusts be destroyed. Now, Mr. Bryan is about the only man in the country to whom the conviction has not been borne home that the trusts cannot be destroyed. The rest of the people want the trusts regulated, and the worst of the trust magnates sent to jail. Up to date, not a single trust has been regulated, nor a single trust magnate sent to jail. Officially, of course, the Standard Oil Company, the American Tobacco Company and the Coal Trust have been cleansed in the blue waters of the Supreme Court laundry and hung upon the line as white as snow. But gentlemen who are not stone blind know that this is not so. They know the Standard Oil Company, the American Tobacco Company and the Coal Trust have merely put on masks and gone on with the hold-up business. Therefore, the Socialist predictions of seventy years ago have all been verified up to and including the inability of any government either to destroy or regulate the trusts.

So much for what Socialists believe Socialism, by reducing the prices of commodities to cost, would do for the people as consumers. Socialists believe Socialism would do even more for the people as workers. Behold the present plight of the workingman. He has a right to live, but he has not a right to the means by which he can live. He cannot live without work, yet, ever he must seek work as a privilege—not as a right. The coming of the age of machinery has made it impossible to work without machinery. Yet the worker owns no machinery and can get access to no machinery except upon such terms as he may be able to make with its owners.

Socialists urge the people to consider the results of this unprecedented situation. First, there is great insecurity of employment. No one knows how long his job is destined to last. It may not last another day. A great variety of causes exist, any one of which may deprive the worker of his opportunity to work. Wall Street gentlemen may put such a crimp in the financial situation that industry cannot go on. Business may slow down because more is being produced than the markets can absorb. A greedy employer may precipitate a strike by trying to reduce the wages of his employees. Any one of many causes may without notice step in between the worker and the machinery without which he cannot work.

But worse than the uncertainty of employment is the absolute certainty that millions of men must always be out of work. Times are never so good that there is work for everybody. Most persons do not know it, but in the best of times there are always a million men out of work. In the worst of times, the number of men out of work sometimes exceeds 5,000,000. The country cries for the things they might produce. There is great need for shoes, flour, cloth, houses, furniture, and fuel. These millions of men, if they could get in touch with machinery, could produce enough of such staples to satisfy the public demand. If they could but work, their earnings would vastly increase the amount of money in circulation and thus increase the buying power of everybody. But they cannot work, because they do not own the machinery without which they cannot work, and the men who own it will not let it be used, because they cannot see any profits for themselves in having it used.

Socialists say this is an appalling situation. They are amazed that the nation tolerates it. They believe the nation would not tolerate it if it understood it. Some things are more easily understood than others. If 5,000,000 men were on a sinking ship within swimming distance of the Atlantic shore and the employing class were to prevent them from swimming ashore for no other reason than that the employing class had no use for their services—the people would understand that. Socialists believe the people will soon understand the present situation.

Here is another thing that Socialists hope the people will soon understand. The policy of permitting a few men to use the machinery with which all other men must work or starve compels all other men to become competitors for its use. If there were no more workers than the capitalists must have, there would not be such competition. But there must always be more workers than the capitalists can use. The fact that the capitalist demands a profit upon the worker's labor renders the worker incapable of buying back the very thing he has made. Under present conditions, trade must, therefore, always be smaller than the natural requirements of the people for goods. And since, with machinery, each worker can produce a vast volume of goods, it inevitably follows that only a part of the workers are required to make all of the goods that can be sold at a profit. That is why there is not always work for all.

With more workers than there are jobs, it thus comes about that the workers are compelled to compete among themselves for jobs. Only part of the workers can be employed and the struggle of each is to become one of that part. The workers who are out of employment are always willing to work, if they can get no more, for a wage that represents only the cost of the poorest living upon which they will consent to exist. It therefore follows that wages are always based upon the cost of living. If the cost of living is high, wages are high. If the cost of living is low, wages are low. In any event, the worker has nothing left after he has paid for his living.

Socialists say this is not just. They can understand the capitalist who buys labor as he buys pig-iron, but they say labor is entitled to more consideration than pig-iron. The price of labor, they declare, should be gauged by the value of labor's product, instead of by the direness of labor's needs. They say the present situation gives to the men who own machinery most of its benefits and to the many who operate it none of its hopes. Now. as of old, the average worker dare hope for no more than enough to keep him alive. Again and again and again the census reports have shown that the bulk of the people in this country are so poor that they do not own even the roofs over their heads.

The purpose of Socialism is to give the workers *all* they produce. And, when Socialists say "workers" they do not mean only those who wear overalls and carry dinner pails. They mean everybody who does useful labor. Socialists regard the general superintendent of a railroad as quite as much of a worker as they do the man on the section. But they do not regard the owners of railway stocks and bonds as workers. They regard them as parasites who are living off the products of labor by owning the locomotives, cars and other equipment with which the workers work. And, since the ownership of machinery is the club with which Socialists say capitalists commit their robberies, Socialists also declare that the only way to stop the robberies is to take away the club. It would do no good to take the club from the men who now hold it and give it even to the individual workers, because, with the principle of private ownership retained, ownership would soon gravitate into a few hands and robbery would go on as ruthlessly as ever. Socialists believe the only remedy is to destroy the club by vesting the ownership of the great machinery of production and distribution in the people, through the government.

Such is the gist of Socialism—public ownership of the trusts, combined with public ownership of the government. Gentlemen who are opposed to Socialism—for what reasons it is now unnecessary to consider—lose no opportunity to spread the belief that there are more kinds of Socialism than there are varieties of the celebrated products of Mr. Heinz. This is not so. There are more than 30,000,000 Socialists in the world. Not one of them would refuse to write across this chapter: "That is Socialism," and sign his name to it. Every Socialist has his individual conception of how mankind would advance if poverty were eliminated, but all Socialists agree that the heart and soul of their philosophy lies in the public ownership, under democratic government, of the means of life. And, as compared with this belief, all other beliefs of Socialism are minor and inconsequential. Public ownership is the rock upon which it is determined to stand or fall.

Socialists differ only with regard to the means by which public ownership may be brought about. A handful of Socialists, for instance, believe that in order to bring it about it is necessary to oppose the labor unions. All other Socialists work hand in hand with the labor unions.

Also, there is a difference of opinion among Socialists as to how the government should proceed to obtain ownership of the industrial trusts, the railroads, telegraph, telephone and express companies and so forth. Some Socialists are in favor of confiscating them, on the theory that the people have a right to resort to such drastic action. In a way, they have excellent authority for their position. Read what Benjamin Franklin said about property at the convention that was called in 1776 to adopt a new constitution for Pennsylvania:

"Suppose one of our Indian nations should now agree to form a civil society. Each individual would bring into the stock of the society little more property than his gun and his blanket, for at present he has no other. We know that when one of them has attempted to keep a few swine he has not been able to maintain a property in them, his neighbors thinking they have a right to kill and eat them whenever they want provisions, it being one of their maxims that hunting is free for all. The accumulation of property in such a society, and its security to individuals in every society, must be an effect of the protection afforded to it by the joint strength of the society in the execution of its laws.

"Private property is, therefore, a creature of society, and is subject to the calls of that society whenever its necessities require it, *even to the last farthing.*"

But one need quote only the law of self-preservation to prove that if any people shall ever become convinced that their lives depend upon the confiscation of the trusts that such confiscation will be justified. When men reach a certain stage of hunger and wretchedness they pay scant attention to every law except the higher law that says they have a right to live.

I believe that most Socialists twenty years ago, were in favor of confiscation. The trend now is all toward compensation. Not that Socialists have changed their minds at all about the equities of the matter. They have not. But they are coming to see that compensation is the easier and quicker way. Victor Berger, the first Socialist congressman, introduced in the House of Representatives an anti-trust bill in which he proposed that the government should buy all of the trusts that control more than forty per cent. of the business in their respective lines, and pay therefor their full cash values—minus, of course, wind, water and all forms of speculative inflation. In short the differences in the Socialist party upon the question of compensation are not unlike the differences which once existed with regard to the best means by which the negroes might be emancipated. Years before the Civil War, Henry Clay proposed that the government should buy the negroes at double their market price and set them free. He said this would be the cheapest and quickest way of settling the troubles between the North and the South. The slave owners would not consent, and, eventually Lincoln freed their slaves without paying for them.

When Socialists speak of buying the trusts, they naturally invite the inquiry as to where they expect to get the money to pay for them. They expect to get the money out of the profits of the trusts. That is the way that Representative Berger provided in his bill. It is a poor trust that does not pay dividends upon stock and interest upon bonds that do not aggregate at least ten per cent. of the capital actually invested. Most of them pay more, and some of the express companies occasionally spring a fifty or a 100 per cent. dividend.

The Socialist proposal is that the government pay for the trusts with two-per cent. bonds, and that each year, enough money be put into a sinking fund to retire the bonds in not more than fifty years. The burden of purchasing the trusts would thus be spread over a little more than two generations, but Socialists say the burden would be a burden only in name, since the prices of trust goods could be radically reduced, even while the trusts were being paid for, and upon the retirement of the bonds, all prices could be reduced to cost.

Those who know little or nothing about Socialism believe that Socialists also differ as to the advisability of using violence to bring about Socialism. Never was there a greater mistake. Above all others, the Socialist party is the party of peace. When Germany and England, in 1911, were ready to fly at each other's throats, it was the Socialist party of Germany that assembled 200,000 men in Berlin one Sunday afternoon and declared that if there were a war, the Socialists of Germany would not help fight it. It was generally admitted, at the time, that the attitude of the German Socialists, more than anything else, was responsible for the avoidance of war.

Socialists are equally pacific when considering the best means by which Socialism may be brought about. Socialists are, first, last and all the time in favor only of political action and trade-union action. Wherever there is a free ballot, they believe in using it, to the exclusion of bombs and bullets. Socialists realize that they can win only by converting a majority of the people to their belief. That is why they begin one campaign the next morning after the closing of another. They are busy with the printing press and their tongues all the while. For them, there is no closed season.

Socialists realize that Socialism can be reared only upon understanding, and that the use of dynamite would turn the minds of the people against them for a hundred years. Any Socialist who believes otherwise is the same sort of a potential criminal that can be found in any other party—and equally as rare. The Republican party had its Guiteau and its Czolgosz, but it repudiated neither of them more quickly than the Socialist party would repudiate one of its own members who should commit a great crime.

Socialists, as a party, stand for violence only in the same way that Abraham Lincoln stood for it. If the Socialists should carry a national election in this country, and, the capitalists, refusing to yield, should turn the regular army at them, the Socialists would use all the violence they could muster. While they are in a minority, they are obeying the laws that the capitalists make, but when the Socialists become a majority, they will insist, even with bullets, that the capitalists obey the laws that the Socialists make.

CHAPTER III
THE VIRTUOUS GRAFTERS AND THEIR GRAVE OBJECTIONS TO SOCIALISM

It is an old saying that the tree that bears the best apples has the most clubs under it. Enough clubs are under the tree of Socialism to stock a wood-yard. Some of the clubs bear the imprints of honest men. Some do not. The great grafters of the present day are the most persistent foes of Socialism. The great grafters say, not only that Socialism is anti-religious, but that it would destroy the family. The grafters also say that Socialism stands for free love.

It may be amusing to hear a grafter oppose Socialism on the ground that it is against religion. It may be diverting to hear gentlemen with Reno reputations charge that Socialism would establish free love and thus destroy the family. But such charges cannot be dismissed by laughing at those who make them. Honest men and women want to know the truth.

The truth is that there is no truth in the charge that Socialism is against religion. Socialism is purely an economic matter. It has no more to do with religion than it has to do with astronomy. It is no more against religion than it is against astronomy. Men of all religious denominations are Socialists, and men of no religious denomination are Socialists. Nor is there any reason why this should not be so. The very pith and marrow of Socialism is the contention that the people, through the government, should own and operate, for their exclusive benefit, the great machinery of production and distribution that is now owned and operated by the trusts. Either this contention is sound or it is not. Whether it is sound or not, a man's religious beliefs cannot possibly have anything to do with what he thinks of it.

But while Socialism is in no sense anti-religious, it is in one sense pro-religious. So good an authority as the Encyclopedia Britannica declares that "the ethics of Socialism and the ethics of Christianity are identical." One of the concerns of Christianity is to establish justice upon earth. The only concern of Socialism is to establish justice upon earth. Socialism seeks to establish justice by giving each human being an equal opportunity to labor, while depriving each human being of the power to appropriate any part of the product of another human being's labor. If the Socialist program contains a word of comfort for either grafters or loafers, neither the grafters nor the loafers have found it.

Nor does the Socialist program contain a word of comfort for the Reno gentlemen. Socialists beg leave frankly to doubt the sincerity of certain wealthy men who profess to believe that Socialism would destroy the family by bringing about free love. Socialists say the best proof that these men believe nothing of the kind is that they do not make application to join the

Socialist party. The wives of some of them certainly make enough applications for divorce.

Addressing themselves to the members of the capitalist class, Socialists therefore speak as follows:

"If the preservation of the family depends upon you, God help the family. If the preservation of womanly women depends upon you, God help the women. You are not all bad, but you are all doing bad. Some of you are doing bad without knowing it; some of you are doing bad though knowing it. But, whether you know it or not, all of you are doing bad because your capitalist system is bad. Your system makes those of you who would do good do bad. It makes you fatten upon the labor of children, because your competitors are fattening upon the labor of children. It makes you fatten upon the labor of women, because your competitors are fattening upon the labor of women. It makes you fatten upon the labor of men because your competitors are fattening upon the labor of men. It makes you keep men, women and children poor, because in no other way could you become rich.

"And you are the ones who are so fearful lest Socialism shall destroy the home. Why do you not worry a little lest the poverty caused by capitalism shall destroy the home? Why are you so slightly stirred by the spectacle of little children torn from their firesides and their schools to work for starvation wages in factories and department stores? Why are you so well able to control your grief when the census reports tell you that more than 5,000,000 women and girls have been compelled to become wage earners because their husbands and fathers receive so little wages that they cannot support their families? Why are you so well able to bear up when the white-slave dealer gets the little girl from the department store?

"None of these facts, nor all of these facts seem to suggest to you wealthy gentlemen who are opposing Socialism that the conditions under which you have become rich are doing anything to disrupt the family or to bring about free love. But you profess to be stunned to a stare when Socialists present a program that is devoted to the single purpose of preventing you, who do no useful labor, from robbing those who do it all. If you have other grounds for opposing Socialism, state them. But in the name of common decency, don't come forward as the protectors of women and children. Your hands are not clean."

Socialists contend that Socialism would do more to purify, glorify and vivify the family than capitalism has ever done or can do. Their reasoning takes this form:

Unless poverty is good for the family, capitalism is not good for the family, because capitalism means poverty or the fear of poverty for all but a few and can never mean anything else. Capitalism can never mean anything else because capitalism is essentially parasitical in its nature. It lives and can live only by preying upon the working class.

If plenty for everybody, without too much or too little for anybody will purify, glorify and vivify the family, Socialism will purify, glorify and vivify it. Socialism will place all of the great machinery of modern production in the hands of the people, to be used fully and freely for nobody's advantage but their own.

Of course, the family cannot be improved without changing it. Upon this obvious fact is based the whole capitalist attack upon Socialism as a destroyer of the home. Socialists believe that freedom from poverty would have a profound effect upon domestic relationships. And Socialist writers have tried to picture the world as it will be when all of the hot hoops of want have been removed from the compact little group that is called the family.

They have pictured woman standing firmly upon her feet, with the ballot in one hand and the power under the law to live from her labor with comfort and self-respect, either inside or outside of her home. But no Socialist has ever pictured a world in which woman would be compelled to work outside her home if she did not want to. Such a picture is reserved for capitalism in the present day. Socialists merely contend that Socialism would make women economically independent, by guaranteeing to them the full value of their labor. No woman would be compelled to marry to get a home. No woman who had a home would be compelled by poverty to stay in it if she were badly treated. For the sake of her children, she might do so if she wished, but she could not be compelled to do so. She would simply be free to act as her judgment might dictate—to profit from a wise choice or to suffer from an unwise one.

Briefly, such is the Socialist picture of the Socialist world for women. No Socialist contends that it is a picture of a perfect world. A perfect world could contain neither fools, hotheads, nor vicious persons. The hard conditions of the present world, and the harder conditions of those long past have created too many fools, hotheads and vicious persons to justify the hope that all such persons can quickly be made wise, cool and good. Socialists, with all their optimism, are not so optimistic as that. They have absolutely no program, patented or otherwise, for making people good.

Their only contention is that they have a program under which people can be good if they want to. They know, only too well, that with the coming of Socialism, everybody will not suddenly want to be good. They expect to have to deal with the bad man and the bad woman. But they do not expect to have to deal with so many bad men and bad women as we now have to deal with. They do not expect to have to deal with any men or women who have been made bad by poverty or the fear of poverty. They do not expect to have to deal with women who have been forced into prostitution because there seemed to be no other way to keep soul and body together. Socialists say that if there are any prostitutes under Socialism they will be women who deliberately choose prostitution as a vocation. Perhaps women, better than men, can judge how many such women there are likely to be.

It is this picture of economically independent womanhood that is hailed by the wealthy detractors of Socialism as the sign that the Socialists plan to destroy the home and supplant it with free love. Socialists say that such conclusions can be based only upon these assumptions:

That nothing but poverty keeps women from being "free-lovers."

That if women were given the power to support themselves decently and comfortably outside of the home, they would at once desert their children, their husbands and "destroy the family."

Socialists believe women can safely be trusted with enough money to live on. Yet the word "trust," as here used, is not quite the word. Socialists do not believe it is within their province either to trust or to distrust women. Socialists believe economic independence is a right that women should demand and get, rather than a privilege that man should grant or deny, as he may see fit. If women do well with economic independence, well and good. If they do ill with it, still well and good. If they have not yet learned to use economic independence, they cannot begin learning too quickly, nor can they learn except by trying to use it.

In any event, Socialists do not claim the right of guardianship over women. They do not believe any human being, regardless of sex, has a right to coerce another when that other is not invading the rights of some other. They believe that women to-day are being coerced. Coerced by poverty. Coerced by fear of poverty. Coerced by men who presume upon their own economic independence and the economic dependence of women. They cite, as proof of their beliefs, the growing number of divorces, together with the fact that women are the applicants for most of the divorces.

And, the astounding circumstance about all of this is that because Socialists hold these views, they are denounced by rich grafters and their retainers as "destroyers of the family," and "free-lovers."

The Socialists have said no more than Herbert Spencer said about the folly of trying to promote happiness with coercion. They say that weakness pitted against strength and dependence against independence invite coercion—no more in a family of nations than in a family of individuals; that a woman whose economic dependence prevents her from doing what all of her instincts call upon her to do is coerced. Here is what Herbert Spencer says in *Social Statics* (p. 76):

"Command is a blight to the affections. Whatsoever of beauty—whatsoever of poetry there is in the passion that unites the sexes, withers up and dies in the cold atmosphere of authority. Native as they are to such widely-separated regions of our nature, Love and Coercion cannot possibly flourish together. Love is sympathetic; Coercion is callous. Love is gentle; Coercion is harsh. Love is self-sacrificing; Coercion is selfish. How then can they co-exist? It is the property of the first to attract, while it is that of the last to repel; and, conflicting as they do, it is the constant tendency of each to destroy the other. Let whoever thinks the two compatible imagine himself acting the master over his betrothed. Does he believe that he could do this without any injury to the subsisting relationship? Does he not know rather that a bad effect would be produced upon the feelings of both by the assumption of such an attitude? And, confessing this as he must, is he superstitious enough to suppose that the going through of a form of word will render harmless that use of command which was previously hurtful?"

Nobody ever called Spencer a "destroyer of the home," or a "free-lover" for that. Yet, if Spencer meant anything, he meant that coercion is primarily wrong because it deprives the individual of the right to be guided by his own judgment. Socialists contend that women have a right to be guided by their own judgment, even if they make mistakes. Men do so. Women rebel against the denial of their equal right. They rebel against the coercion that is worked against them by their inability to earn decent, comfortable livings outside of their homes. Socialists say the family can never be what it might be or what it should be so long as this warfare continues. They say that since the weak never coerce the strong, there should be no economically weak members of the community. Men and women should both be economically independent. Each is likely to treat the other better if they are so.

Francis G. Peabody, Professor of Christian Morals at Harvard, has been as fortunate as Spencer in escaping the charge of being a "destroyer of the family" and a "free-lover." The professor is quoted in the press as follows:

"One thing is certain, the family is rapidly becoming disorganized and disintegrated.... Divorces are being granted at an ever-increasing rate. It may be computed that if the present ratio of increase in population and in separation is maintained, the number of separations of marriage by death would at the end of the twentieth century be less than the number of separations by divorce....

"Owing to industrial life, the importance of the family is already enormously lessened. Once every form of industry went on within the family circle, but as the methods of the great industry are substituted for work done in the home, the economic usefulness of the family is practically outgrown."

Then, painting a picture of the world to come, as he sees it, the professor said:

"Thus with the coming of the social state, family unity will be for a higher end. The wife, being no longer doomed to household drudgery, will have the greater blessing of economic equality. Children will be cared for by the community under healthful and uniform conditions, and we shall arrive at what has been called the happy time when continuity of society no longer depends upon the private nursery."

But what Professor Peabody has said, or what Socialists have said with regard to the next step in the evolution of the family is a little beside the point, and is mentioned so at length only because the detractors of Socialism make so much of it. The point is: *Ought the world if it can, to get rid of poverty, and will Socialism do it?* If Socialism will rid the world of poverty, ought we to retain poverty to keep women good? Who knows that economic independence would make women bad? The grafters intimate that they know. But who believes the grafters? The grafters say the present status of the family is so good that we should be content to remain poor in order to preserve it. Professor Peabody says the present status of the family is so bad that it is falling to pieces. The professor has proof of his statement in every divorce court. The grafters have proof of their statement in no court, nor anywhere else.

Besides, the testimony of the grafters is properly subject to suspicion. If Socialism would remove poverty it would also remove the grafters. If Socialism would not remove poverty or the grafters, but would bring about free love, do you believe the grafters would oppose it? Is it not more likely that the grafters believe Socialism would remove both poverty and themselves and that they are trying to throw a scare into the people by howling about the threatened destruction of the family? If not, why do not the grafters themselves do something to stop their own destruction of the family? A $100 bill will make more happiness in a home than a sermon against Socialism. Why don't they give up their dividends and let the workers have what they produce? Why don't they drum Professor Peabody out of Harvard? If the Socialists are free-lovers, Professor Peabody is a free-lover. Why don't they put him out? Is it because he does not also advocate Socialism?

"Ah," say the grafters, "but the lives of Socialists do not bear out their protestations of devotion to the family. Look at the 'affinities' that some of them have had."

"Quite true," say the Socialists, "but one affinity does not make a fire, nor do two make a forest. What if one or two Socialists of more or less prominence have been divorced? Are affinities and divorces unknown among Democrats and Republicans? Is the percentage of divorces greater in Socialist families than it is in Democratic or Republican families? Where is your proof? What have you got on Debs? What have you got on Berger? What have you got on Seidel, the former Socialist Mayor of Milwaukee? These men are in the limelight. If they should make a mismove, you would blazon it. What do you know against them?"

The foregoing pretty well sums up the situation, so far as the free-love and destroying-the-family charges are concerned. There is nothing in them. Socialists are trying to eradicate poverty *now*. They have no other immediate concern. If the eradication of poverty should send the world to hell, the Socialists, if they can, will send the world to hell. They do not believe anything that can be kept only with poverty is worth keeping. Their observation has taught them that poverty is always and everywhere a curse. They believe no other curse is nearly so great except the curse of excessive riches.

Let us now pass to objections to Socialism that are both pertinent and honest. It is the common belief of those who do not understand Socialism that, under a Socialist form of government, the government would do everything and the people could therefore do nothing; that "everybody would be held down to a dead level," and that as a consequence of the individual's inability to rise, nobody would have an incentive to work.

Here are several kindred objections rolled into one. Let us pick them to pieces and see what is in them.

Let it be conceded that under Socialism the government would own and operate all of the great industries. What of it? The people would do precisely what they are doing now, except that they would do it through the government for themselves, instead of through capitalists for themselves and the capitalists. The people are now engaged in useful labor. A small body of parasites are appropriating much that the people produce. Under Socialism, the parasites will have to go to work. The people will simply continue to work, though under better conditions and for a greater return than they now receive.

Now, let us see just what is meant by "keeping everybody upon a dead level." As the world stands to-day, people differ chiefly as to wealth and to intellect. If one person is not on a "dead level" with another it is because he is more intelligent or more stupid than that other, or because he is richer or poorer. Nobody, of course, believes that Socialism or anything else could put Edison on a dead level with the boss of Tammany Hall. If Socialism is to establish a dead level, it must therefore be by establishing equality as to wealth.

Capitalism has pretty nearly done that already. The great bulk of the world is poor, living from hand to mouth, worrying about the increased cost of living, and going to the grave as empty-handed as when it came into the world. Only a few have any money, beyond their immediate needs, and as a rule that few is composed of men who perform no useful labor. Here and there is a man who combines a little useful labor with a great deal of cogitation as to how he can appropriate something that somebody else has produced. He may have enough to cause him to mortgage his house to buy an automobile, and to make a little pretence of affluence. But financially he is a faker and he knows it. On the other hand, the men who are not financial fakers are not workers. That is to say, either they do no work that is useful to society, or the work they do that is useful justifies but a small part of their incomes.

To illustrate: The owner of a great industry devotes his time to the management of that industry. So far as his managerial activities pertain to the production and distribution of his product, they are socially useful. So far as they pertain to obtaining a profit for himself upon that product they are not socially useful. The value of the socially useful part of his activities may be approximately measured by what he would pay another man for managing the manufacturing and distributing end of his business. The extent to which he is a parasite upon the community may be approximately measured by the difference between his net income from the industry and the sum he would pay another man to manage the manufacturing and distributing end of his business. A hired manager might receive $5,000 a year. The capitalist proprietor may receive $50,000 a year or he may receive nothing—he is in a gambler's game and must take a gambler's chances. If he receives $50,000 a year $45,000 of it is because he owns the machinery. If he did not own the machinery, he himself would be compelled to hire out as a manager at $5,000 a year. In other words, $45,000 a year is the price that the workers pay the capitalist for the privilege of working with his machinery. Socialists therefore contend that we are already on a dead level of wealth, except as to the fact that we have permitted a few who do little or no useful labor to rise above those who do nothing else.

Socialists, however, are not opposed in principle to the economic dead level, and they do not believe anybody else is. If it were desirable that each human being should have a billion dollars, and, by pressing a button, each human being could have a billion dollars, Socialists do not believe there would be an extended Alphonse and Gaston performance over the ceremony of pressing the button. Socialists are opposed only to a dead level that is so nearly level with the hunger line. They want to raise the level to the point where it will comfort, not alone the stomach, but the heart and the brain.

Now, mind you, Socialists have no patented wage scales that they intend to force upon the people. If Socialism stands for anything, it stands for the expression of popular will, and therefore it will be for the people to say, when Socialism comes, whether the manager of a railway system shall receive greater compensation than a train conductor on that system. I do not fear contradiction when I say almost every Socialist believes extraordinary ability should be rewarded with extraordinary compensation—not $10,000 a month for the manager of a railway system that pays its conductors $100 a month, but enough more than the conductor to show that the manager's services are appreciated at their worth. Socialists would also give garbage men and sewer diggers extraordinary wages, on the theory that their work is vitally necessary to everybody else and extremely disagreeable to themselves.

But to satisfy those who want the dead level objection analyzed to the bone, suppose everybody were to receive equal compensation? Should we not have less injustice in the world than we have now? Should we have any suffering from hunger and cold? Should we have so many crimes due to poverty? Should we have any women forced into prostitution by poverty? Should we have a single human being upon the face of the earth haunted by the constant fear that he could not get work and could not get food?

We have all of these evils now. Are they worth thinking about? Are they serious enough to justify us in trying to be rid of them? Granted, for the sake of argument, that we cannot get rid of them without doing an injustice to the railroad manager who would be paid no more than a conductor—is it not better to do injustice to an occasional person who would still be treated as well as any of the others, than to compel all the others to endure present conditions? If not, the "good of the greatest number" is a fallacy, and majority rule is a crime.

But would anyone question either the right or the expediency of such action if the situation were reversed? Suppose that the present system under which a few men own almost everything had made almost everybody rich. Suppose the few who were not rich—corresponding in numbers to the present capitalist class—were to demand that the rules of the game be so changed that they could be made rich by making everyone else poor. Let us suppose, even, that the few were to say that the present system, while it worked satisfactorily for everybody else, worked an injustice to them. Let us go farther and say that the mere handful of objectors were right in such contention. Would the 95 per cent. of the people who were prospering under the system nevertheless voluntarily overturn it and impoverish themselves merely that 5 per cent. might become wealthy?

But there is still another side to the "dead level" objection. Is not enough enough? Who but a glutton wants more food than he should eat? Who but a fop wants more clothing than he needs to wear? Who but a man who has been pampered with riches, or spoiled by the envy that riches so often produce, wants more than a comfortable, roomy, sanitary house in which to live? Does the possession of more things than these make the few who have them happier?

Socialists doubt it. If they did not doubt it, they would still be against conditions that give such advantages to a few who are not socially useful while denying even ordinary comforts to everyone else. And, right here, Socialists again ask these questions: "Even if such luxuries be conceded as advantages, are we not paying too great a price to give them to a few? Is it well that so many should have no home in order that a few should have many homes? And, if there is to be any difference in homes, ought not the difference to be in favor of those who are most useful instead of those who are the most predatory?"

Socialists contend that under Socialism, everybody could not only have work all the time, but that everybody could live as well as now does the man whose income is $5,000 a year. They point to the fact that the man who now spends $5,000 a year on his living, does not consume the products of very much human labor. He has a comfortable house, but comfortable, sanitary houses are not hard to build. Machinery makes almost all of the materials that go into them, and makes them cheaply. And a house properly built lasts a lifetime.

The $5,000–a-year man and his family also eat some food. But the flour is made with machinery at low cost, as are also many other articles. The raw materials come from the earth at the cost of human labor, but the profits that are added to them by capitalists represent no sort of labor.

So is it with clothing, furniture and everything else that the $5,000–a-year man and his family consume. Everything is made cheaply and rapidly with machinery. The workers who make these things get little. The consumer pays much. The difference between the cost of making and the selling price is what eats up a large part of the $5,000. Socialists believe that by cutting out all of this difference and cutting out enforced idleness, everybody could live as well as the $5,000–man now lives. This is only an approximation, of course.

Now we come to the question of rising. What chance would a man have to rise under Socialism?

Let us see, first, what is meant by rising. A man can rise with his fellows or he can rise without them. I am speaking now, of course, only of rising in the financial scale. Habits of thought have been inculcated in us which too often prevent us from thinking of rising in any other way. When we think of bettering our condition, we usually think in terms of money. We seldom think in terms of greater leisure and greater freedom to do the things that make life really worth while; knowing that rich men are usually the slaves of their money, we nevertheless want to be slaves.

Socialism is not intended to help the man who wants to rise financially above his fellows. It throws out no bait to him. A few men will undoubtedly rise a little above their fellows during the early stages of Socialism, but they will not rise very much and there will not be very many of them. Socialism is for all, not for a few. It is devoted to the task of raising the financial standing of everybody who does useful labor and lowering the financial standing of everybody who does not. Socialists say that if Socialism were otherwise, it would be no better than the lottery which is provided by the capitalist system. Socialists do not believe in the lottery principle. They have observed that the gentlemen who run lotteries, rather than the ones who play them, wear the diamonds. Nor does the fact that an occasional washerwoman draws $22,000 with which she knows not what to do, change their minds about the game.

See what a game it is that we are now playing. We teach our small boys that this is a country of glorious opportunities. In picturing the possibilities before them, we know no bounds. We go even to the brink of the ultimate and look over. Away in the distance, we see the White House, and point to it. "There," we say to our boys, "there is where you may some day be. Each of you has a chance to be President. And, if you should not be President, each of you has a chance to be a Rockefeller or a Carnegie. Carnegie began as a bobbin boy. Rockefeller began as a clerk in an oil store. If you are honest and industrious, perhaps you can do as much."

Now, what are the facts? Not one of those boys has much more chance of becoming the President than a ring-tailed monkey has of becoming Caruso. It is not that the boys are worthless—they may have in them better timber than any past President ever contained. But unless we shorten the Presidential term, and shorten it a good deal, we cannot accommodate very many of the lads with the use of the White House. During the next eighty years, even if no President shall serve more than one term, there can be no more than twenty Presidents. During the same time—if we go on repeating such foolishness—perhaps a billion boys will be solemnly assured that each of them has a chance to be President, though, as a matter of fact, only twenty boys can cash in on their chances.

Do we never consider how ridiculous we make ourselves? Do we never fear the crushing question that some bright boy some day will ask: "Dad, just how much do you think twenty chances in a billion are worth?"

I mention this only to show at what an early age we begin to hold out to our boys false hopes of the future. I cannot attempt to explain the fact that no boy asks his father why, in such a country of glorious possibilities as this, he contents himself with driving a truck—but that does not matter. The point is that we go on fooling the boys until they are old enough to know better. They are not very old when this time comes. The world teaches them young. It is the exceptionally stupid young man who does not know, at the age of twenty-five, that the chances against him in playing for a Presidency, a Rockefellership, or a Carnegieship are infinitely greater than would have been the chances against him, if he had lived two generations earlier and played the Louisiana Lottery. Beside such a prospect, the chance of winning a fortune at the race track looks like a certainty. Yet we drove the Louisiana Lottery from the country because it was such a delusion that it amounted to a swindle, and we are beginning to drive the race tracks out of the country for the same reason.

Socialists believe it would be better not to promise so much and to perform more. They believe it would be better to promise each industrious man approximately the present comfort-equivalent of $5,000 a year *and give it to him*, than to hold out to him the hope of great riches and give him, instead, great poverty or great uneasiness because of the fear of poverty.

The Socialists may be wrong in all of this, but they cheerfully place the burden of proof that the world is well upon those who make the claim that it is well. They ask the capitalists to find more than the exceptional, rare man who has realized more than a fraction of the promises that were held out to him in his youth. For every such man that the capitalists may produce, the Socialists will undertake to find twenty men who are living from hand to mouth, either in poverty or in the fear of poverty.

Such is the Socialist position with regard to "rising" in the world. So far as Socialists are able to discover, all of the rising that most persons do is done in the early morning—about an hour before the 7 o'clock whistle blows.

"Early to bed and early to rise" is not in violation of the Socialist constitution, but Socialists respectfully contend that the rising should be made worth while. And, they also contend that if the people must be promised something to make them rise, it is better, in the long run, to promise something and give it to them than to promise more and not give it to them. The best that can be said for the latter plan is that it has been a long time tried and until recently has worked satisfactorily for those who made the promises they failed to keep.

CHAPTER IV
WHY SOCIALISTS PREACH DISCONTENT

Rich men tell poor men to beware of Socialism because Socialists preach discontent. Rich men also tell poor men to beware of Socialism because Socialists "preach the class struggle," and try to "array class against class," politically.

It is all true. Socialists do these things. They make no bones about doing them. They say they would feel ashamed of themselves if they did not do them. If they had a thousand times the power they have, they would do these things a thousand times harder than they do. Just so rapidly as they gain power, they are doing these things harder.

What is it that they do? Let us see.

Socialists preach discontent. Discontent with what? Discontent with home? Discontent with children? Discontent with friends? Discontent with honest labor? Discontent with ambition? Discontent with life as a whole? Why, nothing of the kind.

Socialists preach discontent only with poverty that is made by robbery, and the ills that follow in its wake.

The Hon. Charles Russell, of England, said in 1912 that 12,000,000 of England's 45,000,000 population were on the verge of starvation—shall we be satisfied with that?

A recent investigation into the causes of the shockingly high rate of infant mortality in Germany[1] shows that "the children of poverty hunger before they are born. They come into the world ill-developed, weaker than the children of plenty, and with such low resistant powers that infant mortality rages in their ranks like an epidemic." Shall we be satisfied with that?

1. "The Proletarian Child," by Albert Langon, published in Berlin.

Here in the United States millions of men cannot get work, while millions of men, women and children are compelled to work for starvation wages. Shall we be satisfied with that?

The census reports show that most people do not own the roofs over their heads, having nothing but the clothes upon their backs and their meager furniture. Shall we be satisfied with that?

We are creating wealth rapidly, but what we make is concentrating into so few hands that a few men hold us as in the hollow of their hands, telling us whether we may work, telling us what wages we shall receive if we work, telling us how much we shall pay for meat, sugar, lumber, clothing, salt and steel. Shall we be satisfied with that?

The Stanley Steel Committee's investigations showed that, by a system of interlocking directorates, eighteen men control thirty-five billions of industrial property—a third of the entire national wealth. Shall we be satisfied with that?

In times of industrial depression more than 5,000,000 men who want to work are refused the right to do so, because the few men who control everything cannot see a profit for themselves in letting 5,000,000 men work to support themselves. Shall we be satisfied with that?

The cost of living, mounting higher and higher, is crowding an increasing number of unorganized workers into the bottomless pit in which men, women and children suffer the tortures of hell. Shall we be satisfied with that?

Mr. Morgan, with the tremendous money-power that is behind him, is a greater power in this country than the President of the United States, or the Congress of the United States. Shall we be satisfied with that?

Some gentlemen are satisfied with these facts, but Socialists are not. They are preaching discontent. Should we not be worthy of your scorn and contempt if we did not preach discontent? If such discontent is wrong, contentment with the facts against which Socialists cry out must be right. Who has both the candor and the effrontery to say that contentment with such facts is right? Should we be contented with the woolen mill owners of New England who, fattening upon high Republican tariffs, starve men, women and little children with low wages? Should we be contented with the cotton-mill owners of the South, who, under the protection of Democratic state administrations, fill both their mills and the graveyards with little children? Should we be contented with a world in which a few own everything and the rest do everything—a world in which the worker is but a fleeing fugitive from inevitable fate, owning neither his job, nor the roof over his head?

The cry of this wronged worker has come down through the ages, but never was his hold upon the means of life so slight as it is to-day.

"Every creature has a home home—

But thou, oh workingman, hast none."

So Shelley sang before machinery came. And, oh, the truth of it—the truth of it still! And the pity of it! In these days the inexcusability of it! Yet when we Socialists cry out against it—when we try to awaken the workingman to a realization that a new world was born when the steam engine was born, and that this new world may be and should be for him—we are rebuked by the capitalists because we are "preaching discontent."

Of course we are preaching discontent. We are going to preach it, if present conditions persist, so long as we have breath with which to preach. We respectfully decline to permit capitalists, as such, to tell us what we may or may not preach. We preach what we please without their leave. They preach what they please without our leave. At intervals, they preach a good deal, through some of the magazines, about religion. Big capital is behind the "Men and Religion Forward" movement, and some other similar movements. These gentlemen who are living in luxury off what they take from us tell us to take religion from them in the magazines and be happy. "In the sweet by and by" we are to get our own, while they get their own now. Socialists are willing to stand in on all of the sweet by and by they can get by and by, but they are also determined to make a prodigious fight for the sweet here and now.

Socialists regard poverty, in this day, as nothing less than a scandal. Before the age of machinery there was reason for some poverty. Now there is none. We can make all the wealth we need and more. We could cut our workday in two and still make all we need. Yet poverty is scourging the world as wars never scourged it. In Germany, England, the United States—wherever capitalism has reached a high state of development—men, women and children are pursued to the grave by poverty or the fear of poverty.

Some gentlemen believe this is all right. They believe this is as it should be. With such gentlemen Socialists do not hope to make headway. With such gentlemen Socialists do not seek to make headway. They belong to the rich class who are grafting off the working class. From them Socialists expect no quarter, nor will they give any. The conflict must go to a finish. There will be no surrender upon the part of the Socialists. The Socialist party will never fuse with any of their parties. If the Socialist party were standing still, instead of going ahead, it would stand still alone for a thousand years before it would go a foot with any capitalist party.

Make no mistake. This is all true. You saw the Greenback party wither and blow away. You saw the Populist party swallowed by the Democratic party. But you will never see the Socialist party wither, nor will you ever see it swallowed. Its members are not composed of material that withers or fuses. Right or wrong, they are actuated by the highest ideal that can move a human being—the ideal of human justice. And they are going down the line on their ideal, regardless of the length of the line or of the obstructions that may be placed in their way. After a man has seen Socialism, he can never thereafter defend capitalism. That is to say, he cannot if he is honest. Two or three out of a million are not. Such persons, not infrequently, are hired by capitalists to "expose" Socialism.

But while Socialists do not hope to make any progress among the rich, they do hope to make progress among the working class. Again, I must explain that Socialists do not consider the working class to be exclusively composed of those who wear overalls. Socialists include in the working class all of those who do useful labor. It matters not whether such labor be done by the digger in the ditch or by the general superintendent of a railroad. Socialists place all of those who do useful labor in the working class. Workers are creators of wealth. Creators of wealth differ from capitalists in this: workers make; capitalists take. Capitalists are profit-seekers. The small merchant takes a profit, but it is not the kind of a profit that the big capitalist takes. The small merchant's profit represents only his labor, and is, therefore, really wages. The big capitalist's profits represent no sort of labor. It is such profits that set capitalists and workers at war, because the profits come out of the workers. Socialists call this war the class struggle.

Socialists are opposed to class war. Socialists believe there should be no classes. There would be no classes if everybody worked at useful labor and took no more than belonged to him. But if some men will not work at useful labor, choosing, instead, to make war upon those who are working, who is to blame? Certainly not the workers. They are trying to get nothing that belongs to anyone else. They have never yet been able to keep what belonged to them.

Socialists recognize these facts. They say a class struggle is in progress. Anybody who denies their statement must necessarily know nothing of the existence of trusts, labor unions, courts, lobbyists, crooked legislators, millionaires, paupers, overworked workers, or men who are underworked because they can get no work. Anyone who recognizes the existence of these things cannot well deny either the existence of classes or the existence of a struggle. The dead of this warfare are upon every industrial battlefield, where the fierce desire for profits sends workers to their doom for lack of the safeguards that would have saved their lives. The wounded are in every poverty-stricken home.

Either these statements are true or they are not. If they are true, is it wiser to recognize their truth, or, ostrich-like, to stick our heads in the sand and deny both the existence of classes and the class struggle? Socialists believe it is wiser to recognize the existence of the facts. They deplore the existence of the class struggle, but they can see only harm in closing our eyes to it. If their contention is correct a small body of capitalists are robbing the great working class. If the working class has not found out who is robbing it it cannot find out too quickly. Nor can the working class find out too quickly the methods by which it is being robbed.

It is the advocacy of these ideas that has caused the Socialists to be censured by the rich for trying to "array class against class." If one class is being robbed by another ought not the class that is being robbed to be politically arrayed against the class that is robbing it? Do we not array those whose houses are broken into by burglars against the burglars? Is not the existence of police forces sufficient proof that we do? If capitalists, working through laws they have made, are robbing the workers of thousands, where burglars take cents, why should not the workers be politically arrayed against the capitalists even more solidly than they are arrayed against burglars?

The workers, either singly or collectively, as in their unions, are already arrayed against the capitalists, so far as fighting for more wages is concerned. Without any help from Socialists, we thus have here class arrayed against class. Socialists seek only to extend this conflict to the ballot-box. They ask the worker to remember when he votes as well as when he strikes that he belongs to the working class. They point out to him that he is robbed under the forms of law and that the robbery cannot be stopped until the operations of capitalist laws are stopped. The operations of capitalist laws cannot be stopped until working men stop them. Working men can stop them only by uniting at the ballot-box and wresting from the capitalist class the control of the government.

In this way only do Socialists try to "array class against class." They do not try to array men against men. They do not try to engender hatred of Mr. Morgan, Mr. Rockefeller, or any other great capitalist. Socialists have nothing against any rich man individually. They regard all great capitalists as the natural and inevitable products of the capitalist system. If the great capitalists are sometimes bad, it is because the capitalist system makes them bad. If the particular capitalists who are bad had never been born, the capitalist system would have made others do the same bad acts. Therefore Socialists are opposed to the system that makes man bad rather than to the men who have been made bad by the system. If every capitalist in the world had gone down with the *Titanic*, Socialists would have expected absolutely no improvement in conditions, because the capitalist system would still have remained. Other men would simply have taken their places, and the wrongs would have gone on. Therefore, Socialists leave it to Democratic and Republican politicians to point out "bad men" and say if this man or that man were in jail we should have no more robbery. The slightest reflection should reveal the fallacious character of such comment. Where are all of the "bad men" of the last two generations? Where are William H. Vanderbilt, Jay Gould, E. H. Harriman and the others? They are not simply in jail—they are dead. But who noticed the slightest abatement of robbery when they died? Who will note the slightest improvement of conditions when the "bad men" of the present day are dead? Then how ridiculous it is to say that if Mr. Morgan, Mr. Rockefeller and some others were in jail we should have no more robbery. So long as we have a system that makes men bad we shall have bad men.

Let us now inquire what it is about the capitalist system that makes men bad. We shall not have far to look. It is the private ownership and control, for the sake of private profits, of the means of life. Think how gigantic is this power! All of our food, clothing and shelter is made with machinery. A few own the machinery. The others cannot use it without permission. And, if permission be given, it can be used only upon such terms as the owners offer. Those terms are always the lowest wages for which anybody can be found to work.

Is it any wonder that the few who control this machinery go mad with the desire to accumulate wealth? Is it any wonder that they press their advantage to the limit? Are you sure you would have done less if you had been placed in the same circumstances? I am not sure I should have done less. In fact, I am quite sure I should have done as much, or more, if I could. I say this because I take into account the tremendous power of habit and environment.

An environment of money makes those whom it surrounds forget men. The *Titanic* was not raced through icebergs to her doom because her owners were indifferent to the loss of human life. The *Titanic* was raced to her doom because her owners *forgot* human life. They thought only of the money that would come from the advertisement of a quick trip across the Atlantic. If they had not been made mad by this thought they would at least have remembered their ship, with its cost of $8,000,000. But in their money-madness they forgot not only their passengers, but their own ship. Yet, if the manager of the company had been sailing the ship for the government, without thought of profit, he would have thought of the passengers, the crew, the ship and the icebergs. And if the trusts were owned by the government, the men in charge of them would think of the workers when they fixed wages and of the consumers when they fixed the prices of finished products.

So easy is it to dispose of the argument that Socialism is impracticable because it could not be made to work "without changing human nature." Some men believe we must forever go on grabbing, grabbing, grabbing, while others go on starving, starving, starving. Human nature will "change" just so rapidly as conditions are changed. If one sits on a red-hot stove, it is "human nature" to arise. But if the stove be permitted to cool, one who sits on it will not arise until other reasons than heat have made him wish to do so. Yet, the human nature of the man in each case is the same. It has in no wise changed. It is only the stove that has changed.

Precisely so will the actions of men change when the production of the necessities of life by the government has demonstrated that no one need ever fear the lack of the means with which to live. The very knowledge that the stomach is taken for granted—that with free opportunity to labor, the material necessities and comforts of life are as assured as the air itself—will destroy the incentive to accumulate more wealth than is needed. Even the richest now consume and waste but a fraction of the wealth they possess. Yet they are spurred on to seek still further accumulations, because it is only so recently, comparatively, that the whole race was fighting for the means of life, that the madness for money is still in the air.

The madness for money will not always be in the air. Human nature is wonderfully adaptive. As soon as the workers take control of the government for the benefit of their class, and demonstrate the perfect ease with which enough wealth can be produced to enable everybody to live as well as the $5,000 a year man now lives, the scramble for wealth will quickly subside. It will not subside instantly, but it will subside. A few may grumble, as their industries are bought and taken over by the government, but they will have to take it out in grumbling. They will not even have to work if they don't want to. They will have enough money obtained from the sale of their plants to enable them to live without working. But none of their successors will ever be able to live without working, because no opportunity will exist for anyone to obtain the products of another's labor. Goods will be made and sold by the government at cost. No capitalist will stand between producers and consumers. The people will be their own capitalists, owning their own industrial machinery and managing it through the government.

Those who are opposed to Socialism ask what assurance we have that, under Socialism, the people would be able to manage their government. Others ask why we should not be as likely to have grafters in office under Socialist government as we are now under Democratic or Republican government? Still others believe that a Socialist government would inevitably become tyrannical and despotic, destroying all individual liberty and eventually bringing down civilization in a heap.

Let us answer these objections one by one. And let us first inquire why the people are not now able to manage and control their government.

In the first place, our form of government does not permit the people to control it. The rich men who made our constitution—and they were rich for their day; not a working man among them—purposely made a constitution under which nothing could be done to which the rich might object. That is why the United States senate was created. It was frankly declared in the constitutional convention that the senate was intended to represent wealth. The house of representatives was to represent the people, but the senate was to represent wealth, and the house of representatives could enact no legislation without the consent of the senate. Moreover, the United States supreme court, over which the people have absolutely no control, was created to construe the laws made by congress.

That is the first reason why the people do not now control their government—the framers of the constitution did not intend that they should control it, and the rich men of our day are taking advantage of their opportunity to control it themselves. The second reason is that the capitalist system, based, as it is, upon private profits, makes it highly profitable for the capitalist class to control the government. The robberies of capitalism are committed through laws, and control of the government is necessary to obtain and maintain the laws.

Socialists would abolish the senate, thus vesting the entire legislative power in the house of representatives. They would take from the President the power to appoint justices of the supreme court, and give the people the right to elect all judges. They would take from the United States supreme court the usurped power to declare acts of congress unconstitutional, and give to the people the power to say what acts of congress should be set aside. They would make the constitution of the United States amendable by majority vote, and they would make every public official in the country, from President down, subject to immediate recall at any time, by the vote of the people.

Socialists respectfully offer these reasons, among others, for believing that under Socialism, the people would be able to control their government. Another reason is that, under Socialism, there would be no trust senators or representatives, no representatives of great private banking interests or other aggregations of private capital, because there would be no such private interests.

The reasons are equally plain why, under Socialism, we should not be as certain to have Socialist grafters in office as we are now to have Democratic and Republican grafters. But not one of these reasons is that Socialists believe themselves to be more nearly honest than anyone else. Socialists have no such delusion. Socialists simply point to the fact that all of the present grafting is to secure private profits. When the profit system is abolished, and goods are made for use instead of for profit, nothing will be left to graft for. Public officials could still steal, of course; they could falsify pay-rolls, and probably in many other ways rob the people. But, in the first place, public officials now do little of this sort of clumsy stealing, and, in the second place, whatever stealing of this sort that may be done under Socialism will be punished in precisely the same way that it now is, except more vigorously. Moreover, Socialists do not believe there will be much such stealing, or that it will long continue. And so far as grafting is concerned, when the private profit system that makes grafting is abolished, grafting will be abolished along with it.

Let us now examine the charge that a Socialist government would become tyrannical, despotic, destroy individual liberty, and thus destroy civilization itself.

With all legislative power vested in the house of representatives which is elected by the people, all judges elected by the people and the United States supreme court shorn of its usurped power to declare laws unconstitutional, it is difficult to see how the government could become tyrannical. It is still more difficult when it is considered that, under the Socialist government, the people would have these additional powers:

The power to recall, at any time, any official.

The power to enact, by direct vote, any laws that their legislative bodies might refuse to enact.

The power, by direct vote, to repeal any law that their legislative bodies had enacted.

And the power, by direct vote, to amend their constitutions, both federal and state, any time they wished to do so.

If there could be any tyranny or despotism under such a form of government, gentlemen who profess to believe so are entitled to make the most of it.

Many good persons believe, however, that if Socialism were to come, all individual liberty would be lost. Such persons lack, not only a knowledge of Socialist plans, but a sense of humor. They assume that we now have individual liberty. They do not seem to realize that the average boy, as soon as he is old enough to work, if not before, is grabbed off by necessity and chucked into the nearest job at hand. The boy may have preferred to work at something else; perhaps even he is better fitted for something else. But the pinch of necessity both compels him to work and to take what he can find. He may rattle around in two or three occupations before he finds one in which he stays for life, but the other occupations, like the first one, are not of his choosing. He takes each of them simply because he must have work.

If Socialism would enable the head of every family to earn as good a living as the $5,000–a-year man now gets, the head of no family would be compelled to send his children out to work until they had completed, at least, the high school course. If boys were not compelled to go to work so young, does it not seem likely that, with added years, they would be better able to choose an occupation that would be more nearly suited both to their tastes and their abilities? And if we should destroy the power of poverty to push boys into the occupation nearest to them, should we be justly subject to the charge that we had destroyed, or even impaired, the boys' individual liberty?

Persons who derive their knowledge of Socialism from capitalist sources have strange, and sometimes awful, ideas of what Socialism is setting out to do. They are told, and many of them believe, that under Socialism, the individual would be a mere puppet in the hands of the government, not arising in the morning until the ringing of the governmental alarm clock, doing during the day whatever odd jobs might be assigned to him by a governmental boss, and going to bed at night when the boss told him to.

Suppose we shake up this trash and let the wind blow through it.

Who would thus tyrannize over the people? "The Socialists," it is answered. But who, at that time, will the Socialists be? They will constitute at least a majority of the people, will they not? The Socialists will never gain control of the government until they become a majority—the Milwaukee coalition plan of the old capitalist parties can be depended upon to prevent that. Then what you are asked to believe is that a majority of the people will deliberately go about it to create and afterwards maintain a form of government and industry under which the majority as well as the minority will be slaves.

Remember this: Socialism will never do anything that at least a majority of the people do not want done. This is not a promise, it is fact. A Socialist administration could do nothing to which a majority of the people objected. If such an act were attempted, the majority would instantly recall the administration, wipe out its laws, and assert its own will.

And, also, remember this: If the Socialists, after the next election, were to control every department of the government there would be no upheaval, no paralysis of industry. Everybody would go to work the next morning at his accustomed task. The business of socializing industry would proceed in an orderly, deliberate manner. One industry at a time would be taken over. Perhaps the railroads would be taken over first. A year might be required to take them over. But not a wheel would stop turning while the laws were being changed.

Gentlemen who talk about the blotting out of individual liberty under a Socialist government make this fatal mistake. They assume that a minority would control a Socialist government, precisely as a minority now controls this government. And having made this error they naturally easily proceed to the next error—the assumption that if Socialists were to establish such a crazy government, they would not suffer from it as much as anyone else, and, therefore, would maintain it against the will of the others.

There is absolutely no foundation for this "tyranny-loss-of-individual-liberty" charge. A government controlled by the people cannot tyrannize over the people, nor can the abolition of poverty curtail, under democratic government, the individual liberties of the people. Who now has the most individual liberty—the man who is poverty-stricken or the man who isn't?

Yet Socialists make no pretense of a purpose to create a world in which the worker may blithely amble up to the governmental employment office and demand a job picking a guitar. The worker may amble and demand, but he will not get the job unless there is a guitar to pick. In other words, Socialists expect to exercise ordinary common sense in the conduct of industry. Broadly speaking, the man who is best fitted to do certain work will be given that work to do. It would be absurd to plan or promise anything else. At the same time, the destruction of poverty, and the multiplication of the mass of manufactured goods that will follow the satisfaction of all of the people's needs, will give the workers greater freedom in exercising their discretion in the choice of an occupation.

At this point in the proceedings somebody always inquires, "Who will do the dirty work?"

Socialists do not expect ever to make the cleaning of sewers as pleasant as the packing of geraniums. They do expect, however, to offer such extraordinarily good compensation for this extraordinarily unpleasant work that the sewers will be cleaned. Why should anyone expect that plan to fail, since the present plan does not fail? We now offer very poor wages for this very unpleasant work, yet the sewers do not go uncleaned. Is it to be supposed that the same men who are now doing this dirty work for low wages would refuse to do it for high wages? Most certainly the government would be compelled to offer wages high enough to get the dirty, but important, work done. It is lack of work that now makes men take dirty work at dirty wages. Under Socialism there can be no lack of work, because the people will own their own industrial machinery and will be free to use it. Furthermore, machinery is now doing much of the dirty work, and, as time goes on, will do more of it.

Socialists are often asked what they will do with the man who will not work. If facetiously inclined, they usually reply that one thing they will certainly not do with him is to make him a millionaire. But, really, the question is absurd. What do the opponents of Socialism believe a Socialist government would do with the man who would not work? Do they believe such a man would be given a hero medal, or be pensioned for life? What is there to do with such a man, but to let him starve? I mean a man having the ability to work and having work offered to him, who would nevertheless refuse to work.

But, outside the ranks of criminals, there is no such man, nor will there ever be. Socialists would punish thieves precisely as capitalists punish them, except for the fact that Socialists would not discriminate in favor of the biggest thieves. To answer the question in a single sentence, Socialists would depend upon the spurs afforded by the desires for food, clothing and shelter, to keep most of the people at work, and the odd man who might choose to steal would be treated in the ordinary way—imprisoned.

But the question, "What will you do with the man who will not work?" reveals a strange belief that is held by those who do not hold much of a clutch upon the facts of life. I have a very dear old aunt who believes from the bottom of her honest heart that the great mass of unemployed are either drunkards or loafers. In discussing the problem of the unemployed with gentlemen who are living upon the sunny side of the street, they almost invariably fire this question, "Why don't those fellows get out into the country where the farmers are crying for help and can't get any?"

I was brought up on a farm, and I still remember that not much farming was done in winter. The great demand for extra help comes in mid-summer, when the crops are harvested. During six or eight weeks there is a demand from the farms for more help than they can get. But what man who has a family in the tenements of New York or Chicago can afford to pay his railroad fare to Iowa, Nebraska, or even Ohio, to get six weeks' work?

In the first place, they have not the money with which to pay their fare. These men live from hand to mouth in the city, running in debt during the week, and paying their debt with the wages they receive Saturday night. If their fares were advanced by the farmers who wanted to hire them they would have little or nothing left from what they might earn on the farms, and, in the meantime, their families in the cities would be starving. Furthermore, farm-work is a trade of which these city workers know nothing. They could learn the trade of farming, of course, but they could not learn it in six weeks. At any rate, in panic times there are more than 5,000,000 out of work in this country, and in no conceivable circumstances is it possible that any considerable part of this number could find work upon the farms even six weeks of the year.

The fact is that the conditions of modern industrial life are so hard that an increasing number of unorganized workers are barely able to live, even when they work. The constantly increasing cost of living, brought about by the trusts through their control of markets and prices, robs these men to the limit, and they have no labor unions to increase their wages. Still, they do not refuse to work, even for a bare, miserable living. On the contrary, they are eager to work. So are the great bulk of the unemployed eager to work for a miserable living.

If, under these horrible conditions, men are willing to work, what reason have we to suppose that any great number would refuse to work under a Socialist government for compensation that would enable each of them to live as well as the $5,000–a-year man now lives? Gentlemen who want to worry about this may worry about it. Socialists are not worrying. If, under Socialism, a few dyed-in-the-wool loafers should appear, Socialists are prepared to deal with them. They do not propose to cease their attempts to rid the world of poverty, merely because of the possibility of the appearance of an occasional loafer.

CHAPTER V
HOW THE PEOPLE MAY ACQUIRE THE TRUSTS

Most men are not interested in private profits, because they don't get any. Profits are only for capitalists, and the number of capitalists bears but an insignificant proportion to the whole number of people. Most men are wage-workers, of one sort or another, or small farmers.

Yet we are living under a system that makes private profits the basis of business. If profits are good, business is good. If profits are only fair, business is only fair. If profits are bad, business is bad. And, when business is bad, the whole country suffers, though the country has the men, the machinery and the land with which business might be made good.

Socialists liken the present business edifice to an inverted pyramid resting upon its point—the point of private profits. Socialists have observed that the steadiest pyramids do not rest upon their points. They do not believe the pyramids of Egypt would have stood as long as they have if they had not been right side up. Socialists therefore propose that the pyramid of business shall be turned right side up. They believe it would stand more nearly steady if placed upon the broad basis of the people's needs than it now does upon the pivot-point of private profits.

That is all that Socialists mean when they talk about the "revolutionary" character of their philosophy. They want to make a revolutionary change in the basis of business. They want goods produced solely to satisfy the public need for goods, rather than to satisfy any man's greed for profits. They do not see how business can be thus revolutionized, so long as a few men own all of the great machinery with which goods are produced. Socialists, therefore, propose that the ownership of all the great machinery shall be acquired by the people, by purchase, and thus transferred from a few to all.

Those who are not in favor of this program may be divided into two classes. One class, desiring to cling to the private profit system, is opposed, upon principle, to the Socialist program. The other class, while eager enough, perhaps, to be rid of present conditions, does not believe the Socialist plan is practicable. The reason why so many men believe the Socialist plan is impractical is because so many men do not know what the Socialist plan is. The newspapers, owned as they are by capitalists, do not take the pains to tell the people much about the plans of Socialism. Even so great a trust lawyer as Samuel Untermyer of New York, apparently did not know much about the plans of Socialism until he debated Socialism in Carnegie Hall with Morris Hillquit. Mr. Untermyer, in his opening statement, made the colossal mistake of declaring that the Socialists had no definite plan for transferring the industries of the country from private to public ownership; that no one knew whether they meant to take over all industries, or whether they meant to take over only the trusts, while leaving the small concerns that are now fighting the trusts to compete with the government. In short, Mr. Untermyer left the impression that in the matter of putting their program into practice the Socialists were whirling around in a fog.

Let us see who was whirling around in a fog.

Victor L. Berger, the Socialist congressman from Milwaukee, introduced in the House of Representatives a bill embodying the following features:

The government shall immediately proceed to take over the ownership of all the trusts that control more than 40 per cent. of the business in their respective lines.

The price to be paid for these industries shall be fixed by a commission of fifteen experts, whose duty it shall be to determine the actual cash value of the physical properties.

Payment for the properties shall be proffered in the form of United States bonds, bearing 2 per cent. interest payable in 50 years, and a sinking fund shall be established to retire the bonds at maturity.

In the event of the refusal of any trust owner or owners to sell to the government his or their properties at the price fixed by the commission of experts, the President of the United States is authorized to use such measures as may be necessary to gain and hold possession of the properties.

A Bureau of Industries is hereby created within the Department of Commerce and Labor to operate all industries owned by the government.

Mind you, this is but the barest skeleton of the Berger bill. The bill itself may have no sense in it. But that is not the point. Samuel Untermyer, great trust lawyer and presumably well-read man, said that the Socialists had no definite plan for taking over the industries of the country. He made this statement in Carnegie Hall before thousands of people. And there was not one word of truth in it. If he had taken the slightest pains to inform himself, he might easily have learned that the Socialists have an exceedingly definite plan for taking over the ownership of the nation's industries.

But Mr. Untermyer took no pains to inform himself. Ignorant as an Eskimo of the Socialist program, he just went to Carnegie Hall and talked. What he did not know, he guessed. What he could not guess right, he guessed wrong. He could guess almost nothing right. Mr. Hillquit made him look ridiculous. He was ridiculous. He was more than ridiculous. He was an object for pity. A great lawyer, having a great reputation to sustain, discussing a great subject of which he had only the most meager knowledge!

Mr. Hillquit riddled him, of course, but he did not riddle much because, speaking Socialistically, Mr. Untermyer is not much. But, unfortunately, only the 5,000 or 6,000 who heard the debate knew that Mr. Untermyer had been riddled. Millions of New Yorkers who read the capitalist newspapers the next morning received the impression from the headlines that Untermyer had riddled not only Hillquit but Socialism. "Socialists have no definite plans for doing the things they want to do" was the parroted charge. The charge was not true, but the public did not know the charge was not true. The capitalist newspapers would not let the public know. The newspapers had good reasons for not letting the public know. The newspapers are owned or backed by millionaires who are interested in maintaining present conditions. Socialism would interfere with these newspaper millionaires as much as it would interfere with any other millionaires. Yet it is from such sources that the public receives most of its information with regard to Socialism. It is because of this fact that the public knows so much about Socialism that is not so.

It emphatically is not so that the Socialists have no definite plan for taking over the management and control of the industries of the country. They know precisely what they are trying to do and how they are trying to do it. They have not drafted all of the laws that would be required under a Socialist republic for the next 500 years, but they have formulated certain general principles that, once established, will endure for centuries. I shall endeavor to make these general principles plain.

Socialists want to end class warfare. They want to prevent one class from robbing any other class. They do not see how class warfare can be ended so long as a small class controls the means of life of the great class. The means of life is the machinery and materials with which men work. Socialists, therefore, purpose that the means of life shall be owned by all of the people, through the government.

If this program be put into effect, a start must be made somewhere. Socialists purpose that the start be made with the trusts. They propose that the start be made with the trusts because the trusts have advanced furthest along the road of evolution. The trusts have already sloughed off the multitude of primitive, competitive managers. They are concentrated. Only the slightest shift will be necessary to concentrate the managements a little more and vest them in the government. Besides, the trusts control the bulk of the production of the great necessaries of life. Get the trusts and we shall have life. We shall have food. We shall have clothing. We shall have shelter. We shall have all of these things, because we shall have the machinery with which we may make all of these things.

Long before Congressman Berger's bill was drafted, the cry of the Socialists was "Let the nation own the trusts." Among Socialists, this cry was as insistent and as common as the cry of "Let us stand pat" was insistent and common among the Hanna Republicans of 1896 and 1900. That Socialist cry showed where the Socialists planned to begin. Congressman Berger's bill only echoed the cry and made it more definite. The Socialist cry was "Let the nation own the trusts." Congressman Berger's bill told what trusts were, within the meaning of Socialist demands, and how to get them. Berger's bill declared that a trust should be construed to mean any industry or combination of industries that controlled 40 per cent. or more of the national output of its product. And, Berger's bill also laid down the principle that the easiest way to acquire the trusts is to buy them. Moreover, his bill also sought to provide the governmental machinery and the money with which to do it.

Never mind whether Berger's bill was wise or foolish. Never mind whether the Socialist program is wise or foolish. We are now considering the charge that the Socialists have no definite program. That is what Mr. Untermyer said. That is what a thousand others say. Is it not plain that they are all wrong? Who can doubt that if the Berger bill were enacted into law, the trusts could and would be taken over? The Berger bill is plainer than any tariff bill that was ever written. Any man of common sense can understand it. No man can understand a tariff law. Yet tariff laws are administered. They are definite enough to accomplish what the protected manufacturers really want accomplished. Even those who oppose high tariff laws do not contend that they should be repealed because they lack definiteness.

The simple fact is that the Socialists want to take the trusts first, because they are the most important and the best adapted to immediate ownership by the people. For the time being, small competitive manufacturers would be compelled to compete with the government. If the Socialist theory of production is a fallacy, the small competitive producers would demonstrate it by providing better working conditions for their employees and selling goods more cheaply than the government. In that event, Socialism would fall of its own weight and the nation would restore present conditions.

If the Socialist theory of production is not a fallacy, the competitive producers would be driven out of business and sell their plants to the government for what they were worth. They would be driven out of business, because they could not afford to do business without a profit. They could get no profit without appropriating part of the product of their workers, and if they appropriated part of the product of their workers, the workers would shift over to the national industries where no products were appropriated.

In short, if the national ownership of trusts were a success, the day of the competitive manufacturer would be short. He could not afford to do business with a competitor who sought no profits. And this is precisely what Socialists believe would take place. They believe the national ownership of the trusts would be quickly followed by the national ownership of every industry that is now owned by some to skim a profit from the labor of others.

This does not mean, however, that peanut stands would be owned by the government. It does not necessarily mean that farms would be owned by the government. The Socialists are not fanatics over the mere principle of government ownership. They appeal to the principle only to accomplish an end. The end is the destruction of the power of some to rob others. If there is no robbery, there is no occasion for the application of the principle. The ownership of a peanut stand gives the owner no power to rob anybody. A man who tills his own farm is robbing nobody. Neither the ownership of the peanut stand nor the ownership of the farm gives the owner the power to rob anybody, because neither owner profits from the labor of an employee. But if tenant farming should ever become a serious evil in this country—and it is increasing all the while—the Socialists, if they were in power, would take over the ownership of all tenant farm lands. They would take over the tenant farms for the same reason that they now want to take over the trusts—because the landlords were using the power of ownership to appropriate part of the products of the tenants.

Let this do for the critics who say that Socialists have no definite program for taking over the ownership of the nation's industries. There is another set of critics who say that, if Socialists should ever take over the industries, they could not run them. They say that the change from private to public ownership would bring chaos, that the government, as a manager of industry, would break down, that red revolution would sweep the world and that civilization would probably go down with a crash.

I shall pause a moment to comment upon the lack of humor that these gentlemen betray. They take themselves so seriously. If they were called upon to attend a dog beset with fleas, they would doubtless counsel the dog to prize the fleas as it prized its life.

"Don't bite off one of those fleas, my dear dog," we can hear them say. "You don't know it, but they are doing you good. Each flea-bite increases the speed with which you pursue game. If fleas were not biting you all the time, you might become so comfortable that you would lie down in the sun, go to sleep, forget to eat, and thus starve to death. Remember, the fleas are your friends!"

Of course, the great capitalists who are opposing Socialism are not to be likened to fleas, except as to the facts that they are exceedingly agile and are working at the same trade. But in a season of national mourning over the high cost of living, is it not unseemly for these gentlemen to provoke us to laughter by telling us that, if we were to lose them, we ourselves should be lost? We who work can never save ourselves. We can be saved only by those who work us.

Let us get down to brass tacks. If the Socialists were to gain control of this government to-morrow, probably the first thing they would do toward carrying out their program would be to call a national convention to draft a twentieth century constitution to replace our present eighteenth century one. The convention would abolish the senate, vest the entire legislative power in the house of representatives, destroy the United States Supreme Court's usurped power to declare acts of congress unconstitutional, make all judges elective by the people and establish the initiative, the referendum and recall. Socialists would not attempt to establish Socialism without first clearing the ground so that the people could control their government absolutely.

The work of the convention having been approved by the people, perhaps the first trust that would be taken over would be the railroad trust. It would be a big job. It would be so big a job that no other similar job would be undertaken until the completion of the railroad job was well under way, and the railroad job might require a year or two. I mention this fact to show that it would not be the purpose of a Socialist administration to rip this country up from Maine to Southern California within twenty-four hours from the fourth of March. In fact, there would be no ripping or jarring, as I shall soon show. Everything would proceed in an orderly, lawful manner.

I say there would be no ripping or jarring, because there would be no cessation of industry. Let us suppose, for instance, that the ownership and control of the railroads had been transferred from the present owners to the government. What would happen? Absolutely nothing in the nature of a jar. What happens now when one group of capitalists sell a railroad to another group of capitalists? Nothing, of course. The new owners tell the general manager to keep on running trains, as usual, or if they install a new general manager, they tell him to keep on running trains. The trainmen, if they did not read the newspapers, would not know the road had changed hands.

The transition from private to public ownership would be accomplished precisely as smoothly. The only change would be in the orders that a Socialist administration would give to the chief executive officer of the railroads. That order, in substance, would be: "Don't try to make any profits out of the railroads. Run them at cost. Give the men more wages and shorter hours, and give the public the best possible service at the lowest possible rate and with the least possible risk to human life."

If you can manufacture a riot out of such ingredients, go to it. If you can figure out how such a proceeding would disrupt civilization, proceed at your leisure.

The cards are all down. You now know what the Socialists want to do. Where is the danger?

"Oh," the capitalist gentlemen say, "but you Socialists are not business men, and business men are required to manage industries. A Socialist government would therefore fail."

Mayor Gaynor expressed much the same thought in a statement about Socialism that he prepared for the New York *Times*. Mr. Gaynor's attitude toward Socialism is tolerant—almost sympathetic—yet he asked:

"Who would run your Socialistic government? Where would you get honest and competent men? Would the human understanding and capacity be larger then than it is now?"

Wherever Socialism is discussed, such questions are asked. They are evidently regarded as insuperable obstacles to Socialism. As a matter of fact, they serve only to show how little the questioners know of Socialism.

Socialists do not purpose to establish hatcheries for the breeding by special creation, of a class of super-men to administer government and manage industry. They will depend upon the regular run of the human race for material with which to work out their ideas. But they will approach the subjects of government and industry from a different point of view. The capitalist's conception of honest and efficient government is that sort of government that will best protect him in the enjoyment of the unjust advantages that he has over the rest of the people. The capitalist's conception of honest and efficient business management is that sort of business management that will yield him the most profits upon the least capital. The Socialist's conception of the best government is that which gives no man an advantage over another, while giving every man the greatest opportunity to exercise his faculties, together with the greatest degree of personal liberty that is consistent with the liberty of everybody else. And, the Socialist's conception of honest and efficient business management is that sort of management that produces the most product under the best working conditions at the least cost and distributes it among the people without profit.

In answer to Mayor Gaynor and others, Socialists therefore make these replies:

Capitalists are now able to get honest men who are competent to administer the government in the interest of the capitalist class. Why, then, should you doubt that Socialists will be able to get honest men who will be able to administer the government in the interest of the working class? In either case, it is simply a matter of executing the orders of the employer. Capitalism's employees obey its orders. Socialism's employees will, for the same reason, obey its orders. You tell your employees to maintain the advantage that the few have over the many, and they obey you. We shall tell our employees to destroy the advantage that the few have over the many. We believe they will obey us. If they do not, we shall recall them. That is more than you can now do.

Mayor Gaynor and others also ask if the "human understanding and capacity" would be larger under Socialism than they are now. Positively not. But we respectfully beg leave to suggest that it is not a matter of understanding or capacity. It is a matter of purpose and intention. Men "understand" what they are given to understand. If a man is told to understand the problem of grinding human beings down to push dividends up, he devotes his mind to this task and to no other. If the same man were told to grind dividends down to the vanishing point and hoist human beings high and dry above the poverty point, he would probably understand that, too. And, so far as capacity is concerned, we already have the capacity for great productive effort. We simply are not permitted to exercise enough of it to keep us in comfort. Socialism would not increase the capacity of the human mind, but it would give the nation an opportunity to exercise the capacity it has.

To simmer the whole matter into a few words, Socialism would endeavor to place government and industry in the hands of men who would consider every problem and every opportunity from the point of view of the working class. It is the reverse of this method against which Socialists complain. Capitalists are compelled to consider the working class last in order that they may consider themselves first. The interests of the capitalist class and the working class, instead of being "identical," are hostile. The capitalist class seeks a maximum of product for a minimum of wages. The working class seeks a maximum of wages for a minimum of product. The two classes are at war with each other for the possession of the values that the working class creates.

And, since capitalists control both government and industry, it is but natural that the interests of capitalists should be considered first and the interests of workingmen last.

A little thought is enough to dissipate the fear that a Socialist government would fail, "because Socialists are not business men, and business men are required to manage industry." Let us first inquire, what is meant by a "business man"? Is he not, first and foremost, a man who is expert in the squeezing out of profits? Of course, he is. If he can produce enough profits to satisfy his stockholders, he need know nothing about the mechanics of the business itself. And, so long as business is conducted upon the basis of private profits, it is obvious that the men in charge of it must be "business" men—men who understand the business of extracting profits.

But, with business established upon a basis of public usefulness, with no thought of private profits, of what use would be such a business man? His executive and organizing ability would be of the greatest value, but his ability as a mere profit-getter would be of no value.

For purposes of illustration, let us consider Judge Gary, the chief executive official of the United States Steel Corporation. Judge Gary probably knows about as much about making steel as you do about making Stradivarius violins. He was educated as a lawyer, practised law and was graduated to the bench. He knows a steel rail from a gas tank, but, to save his life, he could not make either. He is a lawyer—plus. A lawyer with a business man's instinct for profits. A lawyer with a business man's instinct for organization and administration.

Back of Judge Gary sits a cabinet of Wall Street directors who, in a general way, tell him what to do. But, like Judge Gary, these Wall street directors know nothing about the making of steel. They are expert only in the making of profits.

Now, a simple old person who had just dropped down here from another planet might tell you that such men could not possibly manage a great business like that of the steel trust. Such a simple old person might tell you that, under the management of such men, the plants of the steel trusts would be as likely to turn out bologna sausages or baled hay as steel. But we know, as a matter of fact, that, under the management of such men, the steel trust turns out nothing but steel. And why? Simply because, below these managers are thousands of highly trained men and hundreds of thousands of wage-workers who, collectively, know all that is known about the making of steel.

Here, then, comes this crushing question. If the Socialists were to gain control of this government, and upon behalf of the government, buy out the steel trust, what would prevent the Socialist President from writing such a letter as this to the chief executive officer of the steel trust:

"Dear Judge Gary: Until further notice stay where you are and do as you have been doing, except as to these particulars: Instead of consulting with J. Pierpont Morgan and your Wall Street cabinet, consult with me and my cabinet. Instead of making steel for profit, make it solely for use. It will not be necessary for you to make steel rails that break in order to keep steel stock from breaking on the market. Make everything as good as you can, sell everything you make at cost, increase the wages of your workingmen and shorten their hours. Do everything you can, in fact, to make the lot of the steel-worker as comfortable as may be."

Would such a letter create a riot? Would Judge Gary indignantly resign and the workers flee?

Would the production of steel be interrupted for a single moment?

Yet, in no more violent way than this would the Socialists take over the ownership and control of any industry. The men now in charge would be left in charge—at least until better men could be found to take their places. Probably, here and there, a man would have to be changed. Not every man who can squeeze out profits is good for anything else. But the men who could forget profits and make good in usefulness—the men who could look at their problems solely from the point of view of the public—such men would be let alone. They would not only be let alone, but they would be given a better opportunity than they now have to make good. Profits ever stand in the way of making good in the real sense. Steel rails that break and kill passengers are not made poor because the steel trust officials do not know how to make them better. They are made poor because it would decrease profits to make them better. Every intelligent manager of industry knows of many things that he might do to increase the worth of his product, but most of this knowledge goes to waste because it would interfere with profits.

Let no man fear that Socialism, if tried, would crumple up because the government would be unable to find competent managers of industry. Every industry will continue to produce men who are competent to take charge of its technical work. The matter of executive heads is of secondary importance. The Postmaster General of the United States, who, almost invariably, is a mere politician, is at the head of one of the greatest enterprises in the world, yet the mails go on. The men who sort letters must know their business. The Postmaster General need not know his. It would be better if he did, of course, but even if he does not the mails go on. So much more important, collectively, are the real workers of the world than any man who figureheads over them.

When E. H. Harriman died the Harriman heirs found a man to head the Harriman system of railroads. The man they found—Judge Lovett—is not even a railroad man, but the Harriman lines go on. The Vanderbilts, Goulds, Rockefellers and Morgans also find men to manage their railroads and other industries. What these capitalists have done, the President, his cabinet and congress, will probably have little difficulty in doing.

Opponents of Socialism make ridiculous statements about the slavery that they declare would exist if the people, through the government, owned and operated their own industries. The workingman is told that, under Socialism, he would be ordered about from place to place as if he were a child.

This charge is no more ridiculous than another charge that is sometimes made, by which it is represented that, under Socialism, the blacksmith would burst into an opera house, demand the job of leading the orchestra, and start a revolution if he were denied the job. The fact is that, under Socialism, industry would proceed, so far as these matters are concerned, in much the same manner that it now proceeds. The workers would be free to apply for the kinds of work for which they regarded themselves as best fitted. So far as the necessities of industry would permit, the applications of the workers would be granted. But, in the long run, the workers would have to work where they were needed, precisely as they now have to work where they are needed, and, then as now, particular tasks would be given to those who were best fitted to perform them. Under Socialism, the worker would have to apply for work, at this place or that place, precisely as he does now. The only difference would be that he would always get work somewhere, that he would work fewer hours, under better conditions, for more pay, and, that, as a voter, he would have a voice in the management of all industry.

Such are the replies made by Socialists to the chief objections that are launched against Socialism. There is another charge—not an objection—that should also be considered. It is the charge that Socialists are dreamers, striving to establish a Utopia. Nothing could be more absurd. Socialists are evolutionists. They do not believe in Utopias, because they do not believe there is or can be such a thing as the last word in human progress. They believe the world will always continue to go onward and upward, precisely as it has always gone onward and upward. Much as they are devoted to Socialism, they have not the slightest belief that the world will stop with Socialism. They believe Socialism will some day become as outgrown and burdensome as capitalism now is, and that, when that day comes, Socialism should and will give way to something better.

The chief contention of Socialists is that Socialism is the next step in civilization, that it represents a great advance over capitalism, that it will end poverty and industrial depressions, and that Socialism must come unless civilization is to go backward.

CHAPTER VI
THE "PRIVATE PROPERTY" BOGEY-MAN

Socialists want the people, through the government, to own and operate the country's great industries. In making this proposal, however, they always specify that they also want the people to own and operate the government.

Upon this slight basis rests the charge that Socialists oppose the right of the individual to own private property. Gentlemen who own much private property—hundreds of millions of dollars' worth—energetically try to frighten gentlemen whose holdings of private property are chiefly confined to the clothes they stand in and the chairs they sit in.

"Beware of those Socialists," say these gentlemen. "They are your worst enemies. They would deprive you of the right to own private property. They would have everybody own everything jointly, thus permitting nobody to own anything individually. Look out for them."

We Socialists say to you: "Look out for the gentlemen who are so fearful lest you shall lose the right to own private property. If you will observe carefully, you will note that they are the ones who own practically all of the private property. You have hopes, perhaps, but they have the property. Your hopes do not increase. Their property does. Besides, we have no desire to deny you the right to own private property. On the contrary, we want to make your right worth something. It is not worth anything now, because you don't own anything and can't own anything. You are kept too busy making a bare living."

The imagination can picture no more seductive subject than the right to own private property. The right to own private property suggests the power to exercise the right. The power to exercise the right a little suggests the power to exercise it much. The power to exercise it much suggests the power to put the world at one's feet; to reach out and get this, whatever it may be; to go there and get that, wherever it may be. Nothing that is of earth or on earth is beyond the dreams of one who owns enough private property. Therefore, the subject may be worth a little more than ordinary consideration.

What, then, is property? Let us look around us. One man has property in land. So far as the eye can see, maybe, the laws of the state defend him in his power to say: "This is mine. I bought it. I paid for it. No one can take it from me without my leave. No one may even pick a flower from the hillside, or a berry from a bush without my consent."

Property in land may be called property in natural resources—property in things that man did not make.

Then there is property in things that man has made. Property in food, property in clothing, property in houses, and property in the mills and machinery with which food, clothing, houses and all other manufactured articles are made.

Now, why should anyone wish a property right in anything? Why should anyone wish to say of anything on earth: "This is mine. No one may take it from me without my leave. No one may even use it without my leave"?

Only that he may fully use and enjoy it. That is the only valid reason that lies behind the desire to own anything. Some things cannot be fully used and enjoyed unless they are exclusively within the control of those who use them. A home into which the world was at liberty to enter would be no home. It might be a lodging house or a hotel, but it would be no home. Therefore, there is a valid reason why each individual should exclusively control the house in which he lives. Such exclusive control may arise from private ownership, as we now understand the term, or it may arise from the right, guaranteed by the state, to exclusive control so long as its use is desired; but, from whatever it may arise, it should exist.

It is the shame of the present civilization that it does not exist. The great majority of human beings have not the exclusive control of the houses in which they live. Their clutch upon their habitations is of the flimsiest sort. The sickness of the father may deprive them of the power to pay rent and thus put them out. The ability of some other man to pay a greater rental may put them out. Any one of many incidents may deprive them of their right to exclusive control of their domiciles.

Exclusive control of the furnishings of a home is also necessary to their complete enjoyment. What is true of house furnishings is true of clothing. Anything, in fact, that is exclusively used by an individual cannot be completely enjoyed unless it is exclusively controlled by that individual.

Wherein lies the justice of permitting one individual to own that which he does not use and cannot use, but which some other individual must use? Why should Mr. Morgan and his associates be permitted to own the machinery with which the steel trust workers earn their living? Why should Mr. Rockefeller and his associates be permitted to own so many of the railroads with which railroad men earn their living? Why should one man be permitted to own block upon block of tenements, while block upon block of tenement-dwellers own no homes?

These questions cannot be answered by saying that the world has always been run this way. In the first place, it is not true. Never, during all the years of the world, until less than a century ago, did a few men own the tools with which all other men work. In fact, it is only within the last 40 years that such ownership has divided the population into a small master class and a vast servant class. But even if the world had always been run as it is running, that, in itself, would not make it right. And anything that is wrong cannot be made right without changing it.

We Socialists are determined to change the laws relating to private property. We assert that the present laws are wrong. We are prepared to prove that they are wrong. We are eager to demonstrate that the poverty of the masses is the direct result of the ownership, by a few, of a certain kind of property that should not be privately owned. We refer, of course, to the industrial machinery of the country, which is owned by those who do not use it and used by those who do not own it.

Our proposal, therefore, is this: We say that all property that is collectively used should be collectively owned, and that all property that is individually used should be individually owned. The last clause should help out the gentleman who is afraid that Socialism would rob him of the ownership of his undershirt. The first clause will help him to own an undershirt.

Please take this suggestion: Distrust any man who advises you to distrust Socialism because of the fear that it would destroy the individual's right to own property. Such a man is always either ignorant upon the subject of Socialism or crooked upon the subject of capitalism. There are no exceptions, for Socialism does not mean what he says it means and would not do what he says it would do.

Socialism would give such a meaning to the individual right to own property as it has never had in all the history of the world. Under Socialism, the individual would not only have the right to own property, but he would have the power to exercise the right. He would own property. If Socialism would not give every head of a family the power exclusively to control as good a house as the $5,000–a-year man now lives in, Socialists would have no use for Socialism. The actual ownership of the house might or might not rest with the individual. To prevent grafters from grabbing houses, it might be deemed advisable to let the state hold the title. But the state would protect the individual in the right exclusively to control the house as long as he wished to live in it, even if it were for a lifetime. If the people so desired, the state might even go further and give the children, after the death of their parents, the same right. But no Socialist government would permit a landlord class to fatten upon a homeless class.

Why? Because Socialists believe that no validity underlies a private title to property except the validity that is completed by the *use* of property. This statement, like any other, can be made ridiculous by construing it ridiculously. Socialists do not mean by this, for instance, that if a man should take his family to the country for the summer anybody would have a right to move into his house, merely because he had temporarily ceased to use it. But Socialists do mean that it is hostile to the interests of the community for a small class to own so much that they can never use.

Socialists believe that the needs of the community are so great that all of the resources of the community should be available to the community. Therefore, they would require occupancy, or use, as a pre-requisite to the perfection of a title. Not that if a man, in spring, were to hang up his winter underclothing for the summer, any neighbor gentleman would thereby be given the right to appropriate the same—nothing of the kind. This statement with regard to use, like all other statements made by Socialists, must be construed reasonably. We simply lay down the principle that it is wrong to perpetuate conditions under which a few are enabled to grab so much more than they can use. Such grabbing hurts. What a man cannot use he should not have. He thereby prevents others from getting what they need.

Besides, what is grabbing but a bad habit? Mr. Rockefeller's $900,000,000, if expended exclusively for bologna sausages, might buy enough to supply him for a million years. If expended for golf balls, he might be able to play golf, without buying a new ball, until he had eaten the last sausage. If expended for clothing, he might be able to wear a new suit, every fifteen minutes, for the next 28,000,000 years. But what good do all of these figures do Rockefeller? His capacity for consuming wealth is extremely limited. It is only his capacity for appropriating the wealth created by others that is great. Every time Mr. Rockefeller's watch ticks $2 drop into his till—but he never sees them. He hardly knows they are there. He has to hire a bookkeeper to know they are there. So far as certainties are concerned, Mr. Rockefeller knows only that when he wants bacon and eggs, with a little hashed brown potatoes on the side, he has the money to pay for them. In other words, the few wants of his slight physical body are never in danger of denial.

Mr. Rockefeller's physical wants would be in no danger of denial if he were worth only $50,000. Why, then, does he want to own the rest of his $900,000,000 worth of property? Plainly, it is only because he is a victim of a bad habit. Some men want money because of the power it gives them, but Rockefeller has never seemed to care much about power. He simply has a mania for accumulation. The more he gets, the more he can get—therefore, he always wants to get more.

And, what does Rockefeller do with wealth, after he gets it? Why, he lets us use it. He invests it in railroads, or steel mills, or steamboats, or copper mines, or restaurants, or whatever seems likely to bring him more money. He does not use any of these properties much. The same freight train that brings him a package of breakfast food brings carloads of kitchen stoves and iron bedsteads to those whose watches have to tick all day to bring in $2. But the point is that while Mr. Rockefeller uses his properties little and we use them much, he is continuously charging us toll for their use and investing the toll in more iron, more steel or more copper. If he charged us no toll, we should have reason to be thankful to him. If he should invest the toll in the necessities of life and dole them out to us, we should, if we were beggars, also have reason to be thankful to him. But he invests his toll in more iron, more steel or more copper—toll that the men who made it need to put blood into their bodies and clothing on their families.

That is all that the private ownership of property does for Mr. Rockefeller more than it does for anybody else. The beefsteak upon his plate is no more secure from outside attack than is the food upon the plate of the poorest laborer. But the industrial machinery that Mr. Rockefeller owns enables him to get, every time his watch ticks, the equivalent of $2 worth of food, or clothing, or anything else.

We stupid people who permit the private ownership of industrial machinery should be exceedingly thankful to Mr. Rockefeller and men of his type. To these gentlemen, are thanks especially due from those persons who believe that the constitution of the United States represents the last gasp of wisdom and should not, therefore, in any circumstances, be changed. Under the constitution and laws of this country, as they stand to-day, Mr. Rockefeller and his associates could legally starve us to death, if they were so minded. Each of them could go abroad, deposit $1,000,000 in the Bank of England, then cable instructions to close down every industry they own, which would mean every industry of importance in the country, including the railroads. No one would have a legal right to trespass upon their premises, and their hoarded wealth would be sufficient to enable them to live comfortably abroad to the end of their days, while the people of America were starving to death.

Of course, the people of America would not starve to death. Law or no law, the people of America would break into the abandoned properties and operate them. Without extended delay, they would change the law, including the federal constitution, to justify their action. But the theoretical possibility of such abandonment is sufficient to illustrate the absurdity of our present laws with regard to the ownership of private property.

When the constitution was adopted, even no such theoretical possibility existed. It is true that we were then almost exclusively an agricultural people, and some of the best families had stolen millions of acres of the most available land. But back of the most available land were untold millions of acres of other land upon which human life could be sustained—land that could be had for the taking and clearing. The factory age had not dawned. Every home was its own factory, in which cloth was woven and clothing was made. Aside from the stolen land which was privately owned, almost nothing was privately owned that was not suitable for private ownership. That was largely due, of course, to the further fact that there was not, at that time, much wealth in the country.

But, viewed from any angle, the unrestricted private ownership of property is a curse to the people and always has been. If it were not a curse, in the sense that it enables some to rob others, no one who is in his senses would be in favor of it. The desire to use property is a legitimate reason for wishing to own it, but the desire to own property that one does not use can arise from no other motive than a purpose to use such ownership as a bludgeon with which to rob the users.

Apply this test and it will be found never to fail. The landlord owns land because he wants to live in idleness from the fruits of those who till the land. The multimillionaire owners of industrial machinery want to own the industrial machinery because they want to use such ownership to appropriate part of what their employees produce. If private ownership did not give this advantage to the owners, the owners would not care to own. If it does give this advantage to the owners the workers have a right to object. Moreover, the workers have a right to insist that such ownership cease.

It is not enough to reply that a man has a right to own any physical property that he can buy. Some burglars have enough money to buy dark lanterns and "jimmies," paying for the same in perfectly lawful coin of the United States. But merely because the private ownership of burglars' tools is not for the good of the people, we have laws forbidding such ownership, and if the laws be violated, we seize and confiscate the tools.

Some day, the fact may dawn upon us that, for every dollar taken with burglars' tools, a million dollars is taken—quite legally, of course—by the owners of industrial tools.

It may be a sore blow, of course, to a man who under capitalism, has never been able to own a coffee grinder, to tell him that, under Socialism, he would not be permitted to own a steel mill. If so, let the blow fall at once. He might as well know the worst now, as later. But if there be those who are interested in owning homes, furniture, clothing, motorboats, automobiles, and so forth, let them be interested in Socialism. Socialism, by no means, guarantees that every laborer shall go to his work in a six-cylinder car, while his wife does the marketing in a limousine, but it does guarantee that Socialism would not prevent him from privately owning all such property that he could earn.

We realize, of course, that this is but a small bait to hold out to a man whom capitalism has given the "right" to own the earth. Among gentlemen who would like to own the earth, perhaps we shall therefore make little progress.

But among gentlemen who have been promised the earth and are getting only hell, we may do better. The time may come when they will tire of piling their bones at the foot of the precipice of private property. The time may come when they will realize that it would be no more absurd to have private undershirts owned by the public than it is to have the public's industrial machinery owned by private interests. Then we shall have Socialism.

"And everything will be divided up equally, all around, and in five years the same persons will be rich who are now rich, and the same persons who are now poor will be poor again."

List to the croaking parrot that has just flown into our happy home. Whenever and wherever there is a discussion about Socialism, that wise old bird wheels in and declares it is all a wicked scheme to rob the rich for the benefit of the poor, and that in no event could it long succeed. Poor old feathered imitation of a human intellect! Brainless, yet not without a voice, it talks on and on and on. Bereft of its feathers and its voice, it might take its place upon a hook in the market place and eventually work its way into some careless shopper's basket as a perfectly good partridge, or diminutive duck. Placed upon the table and served as a delicacy, its worthlessness would soon be understood. But clad as nature clothed it and harping words that some one once dropped into its ear, its voice is continuously mistaken for the voice of wisdom and the progress of the world is commanded to halt.

But the progress of the world does not halt. Those who can think without inviting excruciating pain; those who can reflect without bringing on a stroke of apoplexy, are not compelled to think much or to reflect much to realize that nothing the bird says about "dividing up" is so. Who divided up the wealth that is represented in the public buildings in Washington? What part of the White House, pray, do you own? Do you own the south veranda, or do you own the President's bed? Maybe it is the gilded lady upon the dome of the Capitol who calls you "papa" or "mamma." If not, the wealth represented in the public buildings in Washington has not been "divided up," for you have not been given your share.

Under Socialism, the wealth of the nation would no more be divided up than the wealth invested in the American navy is divided up now. The industrial wealth of the community, owned in common by the members of the community, would be at the service of the community. It would no more be at the service of an individual, exclusive of any other or all other individuals, than the postal department is now at the service of an individual to the exclusion of any other individual. Nor would any man or small set of men ever have a greater opportunity to regain possession of the nation's industrial wealth than any man or small set of men now have to acquire private ownership of the Capitol at Washington. Any man may walk into the Capitol with all the freedom that he might feel if it were his own. But let any man try to sell off a wing as a lodging house and the Capitol police would do their duty. Let Socialists once nationalize the nation's industries and they will cheerfully agree to lay their heads on the block if individuals ever recover possession of them.

Gentlemen who believe otherwise forget that under Socialism there would no longer be the means by which a few pile up great fortunes at the expense of the many. The private ownership of property that is collectively used is the means by which such fortunes are now accumulated. With the means gone, how could the fortunes reappear?

We Socialists are also often chided for what our opponents are pleased to call our "gross materialism." Gentle folk like the Morgans, the Guggenheims, the Ryans, the Havemeyers and others often grieve because our vision seems to comprehend nothing but bread and butter, clothing and furniture, houses and lots and pensions for the aged.

Their grief is perhaps natural. We talk much about those things. We are frankly committed to the task of removing poverty from the world. Material things are required to remove poverty. When poverty goes, of course, a lot will go that is not material. All of the unhappiness that is caused by poverty and the fear of poverty will go. All of the ignorance that is caused by poverty will go. All of the crimes that are caused by ignorance and poverty will go. And much of the vice will go.

Much of the vice? Did you ever consider how much vice would go if capitalism were to go? Did you ever realize to what extent vice is fostered by the profit system to which Socialism is opposed? No? Then read what Wirt W. Hallman, of Chicago, said before the American Society of Sanitary and Moral Prophylaxis. Here it is:

"If any city will take the profit out of vice, it will immediately reduce the volume of vice at least 50 per cent. If, in addition, it will make vice dangerous to men as well as women, to patrons, property-owners and business men as well as to dive-keepers and women street-walkers, it will reduce vice 75 per cent. or more, and will reduce the wreckage of health and morals in much the same proportion."

Socialism will not only take the profit out of vice, but it will take it out of everything. By enfranchising woman and making her economically independent, no woman would be compelled to sell herself to keep herself. Socialism, in this and other enumerated respects, is therefore not particularly materialistic.

But what if it were wholly materialistic? What if its advocates thought of teaching nothing to the world but the best means of supplying itself with bread and butter, boots and shoes, caps and clothing, houses and lots? Do you now require your grocer to teach you ethics? Does your haberdasher supply you with spiritual food as well as neckties? If your house were burning, would you refuse the assistance of the fire department merely because the fire department is exclusively materialistic?

The charge of "gross materialism" is but more sand thrown in the eyes of those who could not be so easily robbed if they could see Socialism. Socialists behold a world that is and always has been poverty-stricken. They say that for the first time in the history of the world it is now possible to remove poverty. And those gentlemen who might have to go to work if poverty were removed rebuke the Socialists because they do not sing psalms while talking about the bread and butter question. Assuredly, no flattery is thereby intended, but indeed what flattery this is. By inference, they tell the world that we are super-men. We could tell the world all it needs to know if it were not for the cussedness that causes us to harp on bread and butter.

The real cause of such complaint is, of course, not that we are teaching the world too little, but too much. We could preach ethics and religion until the cows came home and not arouse a croaker. We could preach nothing until the cows dropped dead and still there would be silence. But when we proclaim the right of the individual, not only to work, but to possess all he creates, the gentlemen who create nothing and own everything fire at us every brick within reach.

Mr. John C. Spooner, once a United States Senator from Wisconsin, but, happily, no longer such, feels particularly aggrieved at the Socialist proposals commonly known as the initiative, the referendum and the recall. To engraft these measures upon our federal and state constitutions would, he says, be an attempt to bring about a "pure democracy," meaning thereby a community the members of which directly governed themselves. A "pure democracy," according to Mr. Spooner, was never made to work on a great scale and cannot be made to work to-day.

Mr. Spooner, who, in and out of office, has always served the rich, is evidently still true to his allegiance. If Mr. Spooner does not know that no Socialist, nor any other person fit to be out of an idiot asylum, has ever even suggested that the government of the United States be converted into a pure democracy, the sum of his knowledge is even less than the sum of his public services up to date. Socialists, and those who have followed us in advocating the initiative, the referendum and the recall merely want to give the people power to do certain things for themselves, provided their elected representatives refuse to do them.

We do not propose to do away with representative government. We do not propose to disband a single legislative body. But we do propose to make every elected official represent us. We do not care whether he be a judge, a congressman or a President. He must represent us. But merely because we are determined these gentlemen shall represent us, other gentlemen like Mr. Spooner seek to make the people believe we are trying to go back to the old New England town meeting days and collect 90,000,0000 people on the prairie somewhere every time a law is to be passed or a fourth-class postmaster appointed. The most charitable construction that can be placed upon the attitude of Mr. Spooner and men of his kind is that they are infinitely more foolish than they believe Socialists to be.

Another point of view is suggested by a Denver gentleman whose letter follows:

"In one of your articles on Socialism, you tell how Socialists would govern—changes they would make in the constitution, and so forth. I should like to ask what you Socialists, or your ancestors had to do with making our present form of government? In other words, what percentage of the Socialists have three generations of American-born ancestors? Socialist leaders, in particular? A very small percentage, I venture to say. Socialism is a result of immigration. Americans still have faith in the constitution of the United States."

When all other attacks fail, the charge is gravely made that "Socialism is un-American" and, therefore, a "result of immigration."

Does it never occur to these gentlemen that the United States are also the "result of immigration"? That the English language, as we speak it here, is the result of immigration?

Would these gentlemen have us reject everything that comes from Europe? If so, why do they not reject the Declaration of Independence, which, though written by Thomas Jefferson, yet breathes the spirit of Rousseau and Voltaire, at whose feet he was proud to sit? Why do they not reject the constitution of the United States which is heavily saturated with the political principles of the English? Why do they not reject the English common law, which assuredly is not American? Why do they not reject the multiplication table, the works of Shakespeare and the wireless telegraph?

Why don't they? Because they are not fools. They are foolish, let us hope, only when they are talking about Socialism. On this subject, their brains curdle. They do not ask whether the principles upon which it is based are true. Truth is not the test. The test is the place where the principles were first proclaimed. If it could be proved that they were first proclaimed at Muncie, Indiana, by a gentleman who was born there immediately after the landing of Columbus—then we might expect these patriots to become Socialists even if Socialism had not a leg to stand upon. But since Europeans chanced to hit upon Socialism before we did, precisely as they chanced to hit upon many another good thing before we did, these gentlemen do not want Socialism, even though it be true.

Well, let them reject it. Let them reject the sun, the moon and the stars, if they want to. None of them was made in America. Let them reject the Mississippi River because it was discovered by De Soto, a foreigner. Let them reject the Pacific Ocean because it was discovered by Balboa, another foreigner. The march of the sun and planets will probably not be seriously disturbed, even if some gentlemen do reject them. Possibly the Mississippi River may flow on. Certainly, the Socialist party in America will not disband. It's busy.

I cannot tell my correspondent what percentage of Socialists have three generations of ancestors who were born in America. I do not know. I do not care. I do not know why he should care. I know some Socialists who have fifteen generations of ancestors who were born in America. I have seen some Socialists when they had been in this country only fifteen minutes. So far as I could discover, they were precisely like the Socialists who had lived in this country, in person or by proxy, for 300 years. They all believed that poverty was unnecessary and that Socialism would remove it.

Either that belief is true, or it isn't. Whence it sprang or by whom it is expressed makes no difference with its truth or falsity. Yet, men who think they can think, write or speak as this gentleman has written. They mean well, of course, but they are suffering from ingrowing Americanism. They are turning their eyes upon themselves and their backs upon the world. If America ever reaches the point where it will reject truth, simply because it comes from abroad, while accepting error for no other reason than that it is made at home, America will not be worth bothering about.

CHAPTER VII
SOCIALISM THE LONE FOE OF WAR

Ask the first man you meet if he is in favor of war and he will tell you he is not. Mr. Wilson is opposed to war. The Czar of Russia is opposed to war. The King of Italy is opposed to war. The Sultan of Turkey is opposed to war. The King of England and the German Emperor are opposed to war. Every king and emperor in the world is opposed to war. Mr. Roosevelt, Mr. Bryan, Mr. Morgan, Mr. Carnegie, Mr. Taft—everybody, everywhere, is opposed to war.

Yet, Mr. Taft, not so long ago, flung an army in the face of Mexico, and dispatched powerful warships to the coast of Cuba. The King of Italy, not so long ago, attacked, by land and sea, the people of Turkey. Mr. Roosevelt and Mr. Bryan, a little longer ago, enlisted in the war against Spain. Mr. Morgan, only a few years ago, helped to furnish the sinews of war with which Japan fought Russia. At this moment, the King of England and the German Emperor are threatening their respective nations with bankruptcy in order to augment their enormous machinery for the slaying of men. And, Mr. Carnegie, having grown rich, in part by the manufacture of armor-plate for warships, is now using some of his money to further a peace-movement that brings no peace.

Plainly, here is something mystifying—a world that wants to stop fighting and cannot. Why cannot it stop fighting? Mr. Wilson cannot tell you. Mr. Morgan will not tell you. Mr. Roosevelt has not told you. Mr. Bryan and Mr. Carnegie seem not to know. No one who should know seems to know. Yet, they must know. Common sense says so. The men who make wars know why they make them. Wars do not happen—they are made. Somebody says: "Bring out the guns." Somebody says: "Begin shooting." Somebody knows what the shooting is about.

What is it about? Be careful, now. Don't answer too quickly. Don't say "the flag" has been insulted. Don't say "the national honor" has been impugned. These are old reasons, but they may not be true reasons. We Socialists are willing to stake everything on the statement that they are not true reasons. If we are right, we are worth listening to. War is hell. During the 132 years that we have been a nation, we have had war hell at average intervals of 22 years. We are already preparing for our next war. We are arming to the teeth. It may not last so long as the Civil War, but it will be bloodier. We have all of the most improved machinery for making it bloodier.

On the sea we are armed as Farragut never was armed. Any of our dreadnoughts could sink all of the ships, for which and against which, Farragut ever fought. And, on land, we are armed as Grant never was armed.

Grant drummed out his victories with muzzle-loading rifles. No rifle could be fired rapidly. No bullet could kill more than one man, nor any man unless that man were near. But the modern rifle can be fired 25 times a minute, and it will kill at four miles. More than that, a single bullet from a modern rifle will kill every man in its path. It will shoot through 60 inches of pine. It will string men like a needle stringing beads. It will literally make a sieve of a soldier. Seventy bullet holes and more were found in the body of many a man who fell on the plains of Manchuria.

Toward such a war—or worse—we are speeding. Indeed, it will be hell. But it will not be hell for the men who make it. It will be hell for the men who fight it. The men who make it will stay at home. Their blood will drench no battlefield. Their bones will lie in the mire with no sunken ship. But the blood of the workers will drench every battlefield, and their skeletons will march with the tides on the floor of the sea.

Good Christian gentlemen who abhor war hold out no hope that war will soon cease. Good Christian gentlemen who abhor war pretend not to know why, in a world that is weary of war, war still persists. Or, if they do pretend to know, they account for the persistence of war by slandering the human race. They say the race is bad. Its brain is full of greed. Its heart is full of murder.

The mind of the race is not, nor ever has been filled with the greed that kills.

The heart of the race is not, nor ever has been, filled with the black blood of murder.

It is only a few whose minds and hearts have been thus poisoned by greed for gain or lust for power. Probably we should all have been thus poisoned if we had been similarly circumstanced—if we had been great capitalists. But most of us, lacking the capitalist's instinct for profits, never chanced to see the easy loot and the waiting dagger lying side by side. The gentlemen who have seen them have made our wars. And the gentlemen who do see them are making our wars to-day and preparing others for the future.

We Socialists make this charge flatly. We smear the monstrous crime of war over the face of the capitalist class. We mince no words. We say to the capitalist class:

"Your pockets are filled with gold, but your hands are covered with blood. You kill men to get money. You don't kill them, yourselves. As a class, you are too careful of your sleek bodies. You might be killed if you were less careful. But you cause other men to kill.

"And you do it in the meanest way. You do it by appealing to their patriotism.

"You say: 'It is sweet to die for one's country.'

"You don't dare say: 'It is sweet to die for Havemeyer,' as many Americans died during the Sugar Trust war to 'free Cuba.'

"You don't say: 'It is sweet to die for Guggenheim or Morgan,' as many Americans would have died if Taft's army had crossed the Rio Grande.

"You don't say: 'It is sweet to die for the Tobacco and other trusts,' as many Americans died during the war with the Philippines.

"You don't dare say any of these things, because you know, if you did, you would not get a recruit. You know you would be more likely to get the boot."

We Socialists, who make these charges, know they are serious. They are as serious as we know how to make them. If they lack any of the seriousness they should have, it is because we lack some of the vocabulary we should have. The facts upon which the charges are made are serious enough to justify the full use of any vocabulary ever made. The facts are the facts of colossal murder for gain. And they are as old as history.

The small rich class that lives in luxury from the labor of the great poor class has a reason for clinging to the control of government. That reason is not far to seek. Without the control of government, the small, rich class would not be rich. Government, in the hands of the rich, is a sort of two-handed claw with which golden chestnuts are pulled out of the fire. One claw is the governmental power to make and enforce laws. The other claw is the power to grab by force that which cannot be grabbed by laws.

One nation cannot make laws for another nation. But the capitalists of one nation may possess property that is wanted by the capitalists of another nation. Or the capitalists of one nation may see a great opportunity for personal profit in transferring to their own nation the sovereignty that another nation holds over a certain territory. That was why Great Britain made war against the Boers. Certain rich English gentlemen believed they could make more money if the British flag waved over the diamond and gold fields of the Transvaal. For no more nearly valid reason, the capitalist class of Japan made war against the capitalist class of Russia. Russia had stolen Korea and Japan wanted it. Korea belonged to the Koreans, but that made no difference. Two thieves struggled for it and one of them has it.

The moment that the capitalist class of one nation determines to rob the capitalist class of another nation, the machinery for inflaming the public mind is set in motion. This machinery consists of tongues and printing presses. Tongues and printing presses immediately begin to foment hatred. Every man in each country is made to feel that every man in the other country is his personal enemy. But that is stating it too mildly. Every man in each country is made to feel that every man in the other country is as much worse than a personal enemy as a nation is greater than an individual. Fervent appeals are made to "patriotism." "The flag" is waved. It is not "sweet to die" for Cecil Rhodes, for Rothschild or any one else—"It is sweet to die for one's country." And thousands of men take the bait.

They bid farewell to their homes. They embark upon transports. They sail strange seas. They disembark upon strange shores. They see strange men. Men whom they never saw before. Men against whom they have no possible sort of grudge. Men who never harmed them. Men whom they never harmed. Common workingmen, like themselves.

But they shoot these men and are shot by these men. They spill each other's blood. They break each other's bones. They break the hearts of each other's families. And, when one army or the other has been crippled beyond further fighting, there is peace. The peace of the sword! The peace of death! The peace that leaves the working classes of both countries poorer and the capitalist class of only one country richer.

Was it not a great victory? Yes.

It was a great victory for the capitalists of the world who lent money to both belligerents. (But it was not a great victory for the workingmen of both countries, who, through weary, weary years, will be shorn of part of their earnings to pay the interest upon the war bonds.)

It was a great victory for the capitalist group who plunged for plunder and got it. (But it was not a great victory for the capitalist group that lost its plunder.)

It was a great victory for the generals, who, from a safe distance, directed the fighting. (But it was not a great victory for the workingmen who, at close quarters, fell before the guns and were buried where they fell.)

It was no sort of a victory for the working class of either country. At least, any victory that came to the working class of either country was merely incidental. Great Britain whipped the Boers, but the British people did not get the gold mines and the diamond mines. The Japanese whipped the Russians, but the Japanese workingmen did not get any of the plunder for which the war was fought. The Japanese capitalists got all of the plunder. The common people of Japan were so poor, after they had fought a "successful" war against Russia, that, within six months of the termination of the war, the Mikado urged the sternest self-denial upon them as the only means of saving the country from bankruptcy. And, notwithstanding the victory of the British over the Boers, the common people of England were never before so poor as they are to-day.

What is the use of blinking these facts? They are facts. Nobody can disprove them. They stand. They stand even in the face of the further fact that some wars have helped the working class. The American Revolution helped the working class of America. But the American working class would not have been in need of help if the English land-owning class who ruled the British government had not been using the government to plunder and oppress the people of America.

But that is only one side of the story. Let us look at the American side. The common people of America gained something from the war. They slipped from the clutches of the English grafters. But they did not get what they were promised. Read the Declaration of Independence and see what they were promised. Read the Constitution of the United States and see what they were given. Between the Declaration of Independence and the Constitution of the United States there is all the difference that exists between blazing sunlight and pale moonlight. No finer spirit was ever breathed into words than that which appears in the Declaration of Independence. Jefferson wrote it, and he wrote splendidly, though the Declaration, as it stands, is not as he first wrote it. Jefferson was so afire with the idea of liberty that his associates upon the committee that drafted the Declaration shrank from the light. They compelled him to tone down his words. But the Declaration as it stands spells Liberty with a big "L." And, Liberty with a big "L" can be nothing but a republic in which the people, through their representatives, absolutely rule.

The people, through their representatives, have never ruled this country and do not rule it to-day. The Constitution of the United States will not let them. It will not let them vote directly for President. In the beginning, the people did not even choose the electors who elected the President. State Legislatures chose them. No man except a legislator ever voted for the electors who chose Washington, Adams, Jefferson, Madison and some others. To this day the Constitution denies the right of the people to choose United States Senators and Justices of the United States Supreme Court. In the few states where the people practically choose United States Senators they do so only by "going around the end" of the Constitution. They exact a promise from legislative candidates to elect the senators for whom the people have expressed a preference. But this is wholly extra-constitutional. If the legislators were to break their promises, the United States Supreme Court would be compelled to sustain them in their constitutional right to do so.

Now, here is the point. Granted that the American Revolution was of value to the American working class. Granted that the ills that followed from American rule were not so grievous as the ills inflicted by the ruling class of England. Grant all this and more. Still, is it not true that if it had not been for the ruling class of England, there would have been no occasion for a war? Is it not true that the English people, if they had been in control of their own government, never would have harmed the people of America? When did the English people, or any other people, ever harm anybody? When did a thievish, murderous ruling class neglect to harm any people whose plunder seemed possible and profitable?

The idea that the people of one country, if left to themselves, would ever become embittered against the people of another country, is absurd. Test this statement by your own feelings. Are you so angry at some Japanese peasant who is now patiently toiling upon his little hillside in Japan, that you would like to go to Japan and kill him? Is there any person in Germany whom you never saw that you want to kill?

Of course not. But if you are a "patriotic" American citizen, you may some day cross a sea to kill somebody. If you believe in "following the flag," the flag may some day lead you into the hell of war. If you believe "it is sweet to die for one's country," you may some day be shot to pieces. But if so, you will not die for your country. Your country wants you to live. You will die for the ruling class of your country. If you should expire from gunshot wounds in Mexico, you might die for Mr. Guggenheim, or some other noble citizen who will be far from the firing line. Wherever you may die from war-wounds, you will die to put more money into somebody else's pockets.

It has always been so. Why did we go to war against England in 1812? Because the English people had wronged us? The English people, left to themselves, never wronged anybody. We went to war with England in 1812 because the ruling class of England, then deep in the Napoleonic wars, were holding up American ships upon the high seas to take off alleged British subjects and jam them into the British Navy.

Such action, of course, was harmful to American pride, but really it did not deeply concern the American working class. Most of the workers lived and died without ever having seen a ship. Nevertheless, the American working class was summoned to the slaughter. My paternal great-grandfather, a humble farmer in the Hudson River Valley, was drafted into the ranks, and to this day I honor him because he would not go without being drafted. And, when the war was ended, the working class of America was worse off than it was before.

So was the working class of England. Some were dead. Some were shattered in health. The living lived less well because they had to pay the cost of hell. The impressment of alleged British subjects upon the high seas ceased only because Great Britain chose to end it. The treaty of peace contained no stipulation that she should end it. Thus ceased this criminally stupid war, which never would have begun if the people of England, instead of a small ruling class, had ruled their own country.

The war with Mexico was so monstrous that General Grant, who fought in it, denounced it in the strongest language at his command. In the second chapter of the first volume of his "Memoirs," after characterizing the Mexican War as "unholy," he says:

"The occupation, separation and annexation" (of Texas) "were, from the inception of the movement to its final consummation, a conspiracy to acquire territory out of which slave states might be formed for the American Union. Even if the annexation itself could be justified, the manner in which the subsequent war was forced upon Mexico cannot.... The Southern Rebellion was largely the outgrowth of the Mexican War."

Do you get that? Two wars caused by slavery. Seven hundred thousand men killed. Twenty billion dollars' worth of wealth either destroyed outright, or consumed for interest upon the public debt, or paid for subsequent pensions.

And for what?

To settle the question of slavery.

To settle the question of slavery that the men who framed the national Constitution, most of whom were slaveholders, permitted to exist.

To settle the question of slavery, which, never for one moment, during all of those intervening years, was anything but a curse even to the white working class.

And, what is chattel slavery? Merely a method of appropriating the products of the labor of others. Who were interested in maintaining it? Certainly not the working class, no member of which ever owned a slave. The capitalist class of the South was interested in it, because its holdings were agricultural, and slave labor was well adapted to agricultural undertakings. The capitalist class of the North was not interested in maintaining chattel slavery, because the investments of Northern capitalists were chiefly in industrial undertakings, for which black slave labor was not well suited. Yet, the North never seriously objected to slavery, as such. Men like Wendell Phillips, who did object to slavery, as such, were mobbed in the North. If the North, like the South, had been, so far as the great capitalists were concerned, an agricultural country, there is no reason whatever to suppose that the North would not have been in favor of chattel slavery. What the North most objected to was the effort of the South to extend slavery into new states, as they were admitted. The Southern aristocracy, in this manner, sought to prevent the loss of its hold upon the government. The Northern capitalists also desired to gain control of the government. When the addition of new free states stripped the South of its political supremacy, the South went to war. The North resisted the attack to save the Union.

Remember, that is why the North went to war—to save the Union, which had been attacked. It was not to free the slaves and end slavery. We have this upon the authority of no less a man than Lincoln. Lincoln once sent word to the South that if it would permit him to put one word into a peace-treaty, he would let the South put in all the others. The one word that Lincoln said he wanted to put in was "union." Lincoln was opposed to slavery, but he was not so much opposed to it that he wanted to fight about it. It was only after the South had fought Lincoln almost to a standstill that he rose above the Constitution and destroyed an institution that was not even mentioned in the Constitution—much less prohibited by it.

That is what the Civil War was about—chattel slavery.

Something that would not have existed if men had not first existed who wished to ride upon the backs of others.

Something that would not have existed if the representatives of the ruling class who drafted the Constitution had not been eager that it should persist.

Something that never for a moment benefited the working class.

Yet, the working class fought the war—on one side to preserve slavery for the benefit of others; on the other side to maintain a union under which white men and black men alike are always upon the brink of poverty.

Seven hundred thousand men followed the Stars and Stripes and the Stars and Bars—to bloody graves. Not one of them would have been killed in war if the common people of each section had ruled each section. The common people never owned slaves. They did well if they owned themselves.

And now we come to the Spanish-American War. We believe it was fought to "free Cuba." We believe it was fought to "avenge the *Maine*." Don't take too much for granted. Even Senator Nelson, of Minnesota, declared in the United States Senate in 1912 his belief that the war with Spain was fomented by Americans who held large interests in Cuba. He also declared his belief that the Sugar Trust was trying to foment another revolution for the purpose of bringing about annexation and thus ridding itself of the 80 percent. tariff that is now levied upon American sugar.

But there is more to the story. To this day, there is no proof that the *Maine* was destroyed by Spaniards, Cubans, or anyone outside of her. For fourteen years the government of the United States did not seem to want to know. The *Maine*, with the bones of 200 or 300 workingmen aboard her, was permitted to lie in the mud of Havana harbor where she sank. And, when the wreck was tardily raised, nobody was able to say that the ship was not destroyed by the explosion of her own magazines. Now, the hull of the old ship is down far in the ocean, with no hope that the facts will be known.

But the interests that wanted war had no doubt of the facts in 1898. Their newspapers thundered their theory every day. The *Maine* had been destroyed by Spaniards! We must "Remember the *Maine*." We did remember the *Maine*, but we forgot ourselves. We forgot to be sure we were right. And, even if we were right, we forgot that the killing of a few thousands of Spanish workingmen would be no fit punishment for the crime of the Spanish ruling class that wrecked the *Maine*.

We also forgot to watch what Wall Street was doing at the time. Read some paragraphs from the New York *Tribune* of April 1, 6, 9 and 20, 1898:

"Mr. Guerra, of the Cuban Junta, was asked about the Spanish-Cuban bonds against the revenues of the island. He replied that he did not know their amount, which report fixed at $400,000,000...."

"These bonds are payable in gold, at 6 per cent. interest, ten years after the war with Spain had ended...."

"The disposition of the bonds of the Cuban Republic has been a question discussed in certain quarters during the last few days, and the grave charge has been made that the bonds have been given away indiscriminately in the United States to people of influence who would therefore become interested in seeing the Republic of Cuba on such terms with the United States as would make the bonds valuable pieces of property." (Kindly note that the bonds would be worth nothing unless Spain were driven out of Cuba.) "Men of business, newspaper, and even public officials, have been mentioned as having received these bonds as a gift...."

"A congressman said in the house on Monday that he had $10,000 worth of Cuban bonds in his pocket, while H. H. Kohlsaat, in an editorial in one of the Chicago papers, charges the Junta with offering a bribe of $2,000,000 of Cuban bonds to a Chicago man to use his influence with the administration for the recognition of the Cuban government."

"Mr. Guerra made the somewhat startling statement that a man representing certain individuals at Washington has sought to coerce the Junta into selling $10,000,000 worth of bonds at 20 cents on the dollar. 'This man practically threatened us that unless we let him have the bonds at the price quoted, Cuba would never receive recognition. He said he was prepared to pay on the spot $2,000,000 in American money for $10,000,000 of Cuban bonds, but his offer was refused.'"

You probably do not remember these items. Perhaps, at that time, like many other citizens, you were too busy "remembering the *Maine*." If so, what do you think of these items now? Do they mean anything to you? Do they offer any explanation as to why this government, after having paid little or no attention to six rebellions in Cuba during a 50–year period, suddenly determined to "free Cuba"?

In any event, remember that whatever Spain did to Cuba was done by the ruling class and not by the people of Spain. The ruling class was bent upon the robbery of the Cubans. The people of Spain did not profit from the robbery. Nor was the working class of the United States helped by the expulsion of Spain from Cuba. The Sugar Trust and some other great American interests were helped, but the American working class was not. The working class had only the pleasure of doing the fighting, the dying and the bill-paying.

The American working class profited no more from the war with the Philippines, which was fought solely to provide a new field for the dollar-activities of American capitalists. There is no American workingman who now finds it easier to make a living because of the generally improved conditions brought about by the war with the Philippines. General conditions have not been improved. They have been made worse to the extent that the cost of the war is a burden upon industry. If working-class interests had been consulted, the war never would have been waged. No working class interest was involved. The workers had everything to lose, including life, by going to the front, and nothing to gain. But they "followed the flag"—and some of them never came back. They stayed—six feet under ground—that the Tobacco Trust, the Timber Trust, and many other great capitalist interests might stay on the islands above the ground.

Look wherever you will, you cannot find a working class interest that should or could cause workingmen to slaughter each other. Nor is this situation new. It is as old as war itself. It is a fact that men of sense and honesty have always recognized. Tacitus said:

"Gold and power are the chief causes of war."

Dryden, the poet, said: "War seldom enters but where wealth allures."

And Carlyle, in this striking fashion, showed the utter absence of working-class interest in war:

"To my own knowledge, for example, there dwell and toil in the British village of Dumrudge, usually some five hundred souls. From these, by certain 'natural enemies' of the French, there are successively selected, during the French war, say, thirty able-bodied men. Dumrudge, at her own expense, has suckled and nursed them. She has not, without difficulty and sorrow, fed them up to manhood and even trained them up to crafts, so that one can weave, another build, another hammer, and the weakest can stand under some thirty stone, avoirdupois.

"Nevertheless, amid much weeping and swearing, they are selected, all dressed in red and shipped away, at public expense, some two thousand miles, or, say, only to the south of Spain, and fed there till wanted.

"And now, to the same spot in the South of Spain, are sent thirty similar French artisans—in like manner wending their ways, till at length, after infinite effort, the two parties come into actual juxtaposition, and thirty stand facing thirty, each with a gun in his hand. Straightway the order 'Fire!' is given, and they blow the souls out of one another; and, in the place of sixty brisk, useful craftsmen, the world has sixty dead carcasses, which it must bury and anew shed tears for.

"Had these men any quarrel? Busy as the devil is, not the smallest! They lived far enough apart; were the entirest strangers; nay, in so wide a universe, there was even, unconsciously, by commerce, some mutual helpfulness between them.

"How, then?

"Simpleton! Their governors had fallen out, and, instead of shooting one another, had these poor blockheads shoot."

That is the cause of war between nations—"the governors fall out." And who are the governors? Nobody but the representatives of the ruling class, who clash in their race for plunder and deceive workingmen into doing their fighting for them.

Now, let us go back a bit. You may recall that I said that the ruling capitalist class uses government as a two-handed claw with which to pull golden chestnuts out of the fire. One hand of this claw is the power to make and enforce laws. The other hand—the power to wage war—is used to grab what cannot be grabbed with laws. Wars between nations illustrate one form of effort to get what laws cannot give. Here is another:

The United States is dotted with forts, arsenals and armories. Far in the interior, where, by the widest stretch of the imagination, no foreign army could come, we see these grim reminders and prognosticators of war. Under the Dick Military Law, the President of the United States, without further legislation, can compel every man in the United States, between the ages of 18 and 45 years, to enlist in the militia of his state and serve under the orders of the President of the United States. The President, therefore, has it in his power at any time to raise an army of about 12,000,000 men and place them in the field.

What for? To fight a foreign foe? Not much. The Constitution of the United States forbids the President to make war against a foreign nation without the explicit authorization of Congress. But the Dick Law authorizes the President to raise this enormous army and to command it.

Here is the question. At whom is this enormous potential army aimed? Why is the land strewn with arsenals and armories that could be of little or no service in a foreign war?

To quote a word from Carlyle, "Simpleton," do you not know that all of these arrangements are made to shoot you if the capitalist class should ever decide that you should be shot? Nor, have you never noticed against whom the state militia is invariably used?

If you have noticed none of these things, perhaps it would be well for you to wake up. The militia of the states is practically never used except to beat down workingmen who have revolted against the outrageous wrongs heaped upon them by their employers. American workingmen do not readily revolt. Nowhere are they any too prosperous. Millions believe from the bottoms of their hearts that they are being robbed. Yet, they keep on. Only when they are ground into the dust, as they were by the Woolen Trust at Lawrence, or by the Coal Trust in Pennsylvania, do they rebel.

Please, therefore, note this monstrous situation:

Under the laws of the land, the capitalists have a right to grind their employees as deeply into the dust as they can grind them.

While this process is going on the national and state troops are quite still. But when human nature, unable to bear up longer, explodes and a few window panes are broken, the troops come scurrying to the scene. Soldiers fill the streets, citizens are ordered this way and that, guns are fired recklessly, perhaps a man or two or a woman or two are killed; the soldiers deny the killing and charge it to the strikers themselves, and eventually the strike is broken.

Can you recall when the militia of a state was recently used for anything else?

Now, we Socialists do not believe in violence, even by strikers. We are supposed to be greedy for blood, but we are not. We do believe, however, the best way to end violence caused by robbery is to end the robbery. We believe it is contemptible for a government to be blind to robbery so long as it proceeds without an outcry from the victim. We believe it is criminal for the government to shoot the victim simply because, in his distress, he breaks a pane of glass in the factory or mill in which he was robbed. We can understand why such crimes are committed, because we know that the same capitalist interests that control industry also control government. But, understanding the offense does not make us approve it. We are against the great crime of war, whether it be practiced upon a huge scale abroad, or upon a small scale at home.

But the President is also opposed to war, the Czar of Russia is also opposed to war, and the German Emperor is also opposed to war. No Socialist can outdo any of these gentlemen in deploring war. The smallest Socialist, however, outdoes any of these gentlemen in making good upon his declaration. Socialists will not go to war. They will not join the army, the militia, or the navy. All over the world this is true. They preach against war in season and out of season. They preach against anything that tends toward war. They preach against dressing little boys as soldiers and calling them "scouts." And wherever Socialists hold seats in national legislative bodies, their attitude is "No men; no money." They will vote for no bill that seeks to draw another man or another dollar into the horrible game of war.

Those who do not understand us, or who do not want us to be understood, charge us with lack of patriotism. If blood-letting for dollars be the test of patriotism, we certainly are not patriotic. We refuse to kill men for money, either for ourselves or for any one else. Nor do we believe that Frenchmen, Englishmen, Germans or any others are less our brothers than are Americans. We regard all nationalities and races as members of the great human family. We want this family to live in peace. We preach peace. We live peace.

But how can there be peace when great groups of capitalists are contending for profits? How can there be peace when great groups of capitalists controlling their respective governments, build great fleets and muster great armies to struggle for trade and profits? How can there be peace when these same capitalists, through their control of government, teach even school children that the warrior's trade is glorious and that the citizen's duty is to "stand by the flag"? Our flag has often stood where it had no moral right to stand. It has stood for the wrongs of capitalism when it should have stood for the rights of the people. Our flag will always stand for the wrongs of capitalism, so long as capitalism controls the government.

In such circumstances, there can be no assured peace. Peace tribunals, like that of The Hague, may be established until their sponsors are black in the face, but still there will be no peace. There can be no peace. Profits prevent. The gentlemen who attach themselves to these tribunals want peace—if. Peace if it can be maintained without hurting profits. Peace if it can be maintained without restraining capitalistic brigands who wish to descend upon the property of others. Peace if it can be had without price.

So war continues in a world that is weary of war. Heavier and heavier becomes the burden of armaments. The workingman staggers under the weight of the fourteen-inch gun. The workingman may go hungry. The gun must be fed.

"Whether your shell hits the target or not,

Your cost is six hundred dollars a shot.

You thing of noise and flame and power,

We feed you a hundred barrels of flour

Each time you roar. Your flame is fed

With twenty thousand loaves of bread.

Silence! A million hungry men

Seek bread to fill their mouths again."[2]

2. P. F. McCarthy, in the New York *World*.

Only one machine can smash this gun, and that is the printing press. The greatest gun can shoot only twenty miles or so. The Socialist press can shoot and is shooting around the world. When the working class controls its printing presses, war will end.

Do you really want war to end, or is a string attached to your wish? If you mean business, you can help end it. But if you want the privilege of aiding in this great work for humanity, you will have to vote the Socialist ticket. It is the only ticket that always and everywhere is sternly against war, as the Socialist party is the only party opposed to the profit system that makes wars.

I cannot close this chapter without calling the attention of readers to a book entitled "War—What For?" by Mr. George R. Kirkpatrick. It is published by the author at West Lafayette, Ohio. Between darkness and daylight, one night, I read it all. I can never forget it. If all the world had read it, there would be no more war.

CHAPTER VIII
WHY SOCIALISTS OPPOSE "RADICAL" POLITICIANS

A "radical" politician, when he is not an utter fraud, is a well-meaning man who lacks either the courage or the insight to do well. He can see wrongs, but he cannot see rights. Or, if he can see rights, he dare not do right. Always, there is some reason why he should not do right. The people are not ready. The time is not propitious. Thus does he appease his conscience, betray his followers and destroy himself.

Abraham Lincoln, during all except the last two years of his life, was such a man. I sometimes feel that this is why so many modern "radicals" believe they are second Lincolns. They seem to remember Lincoln only as he was when he was too small for his task. Mr. Roosevelt, in particular, is suspected of harboring the belief that he is a second Lincoln. In a way and to a degree, Mr. Roosevelt is right. The ground upon which Mr. Roosevelt now stands is broadly comparable to the ground upon which Mr. Lincoln stood before he signed the Emancipation Proclamation. Mr. Lincoln hated chattel slavery, but was willing to end the war with slavery intact. Mr. Roosevelt hates the robbery of man by man, but he shrinks from trying to seize the club with which the robbery is committed. He is willing to pick at the splinters upon the club, precisely as Mr. Lincoln was long willing to content himself with efforts to restrict the evil of slavery. And, Mr. Roosevelt, picking at splinters, is no more useful in destroying poverty than was Mr. Lincoln, when he picked at the splinters of chattel slavery. The Civil War came on, in spite of all that Lincoln did, because he did no more than to temporize with the evil that was destined to cause the war. Mr. Roosevelt, even as the leader of a new political party, is doing no more than to temporize with the monstrous evil of unnecessary poverty in America.

Let us look, even more closely, into the life of Lincoln. The career of no other man of modern times is so well suited to our purpose. We want to know whether a "radical" like Roosevelt or Wilson should be more highly regarded by the people than a revolutionist like Debs or Berger. Lincoln, at different times in his life, was both a "radical" and a revolutionist. His "radical" beliefs put him into the White House. One colossal revolutionary act put him into the hearts of men. We Socialists feel that he nestles a little more closely to our hearts than he does to some others. When Lincoln ceased to temporize with chattel slavery and struck it down, he became one of us. He actually did to chattel slavery what we are trying to do to wage slavery.

The magnitude of this act, as well as the usefulness of a mere "radical" politician, may be measured by what Lincoln's life would have been without his name at the bottom of the Emancipation Proclamation. Tradition has it that Lincoln became a radical upon the slavery question when, as a flatboatman upon the Mississippi, he saw a negress sold upon the auction block at New Orleans. Tradition has it that he said: "If I ever have a chance to hit slavery, I will hit it and hit it hard."

The fact is that when Mr. Lincoln began to get the power to hit slavery, he did not hit it hard. He was a "radical" politician and therefore could not hit it hard. He was against slavery, but he was also against anything that would end slavery. In the phrase of our time, he wanted to "regulate" slavery. Men like John Brown and William Lloyd Garrison wanted to end slavery and advocated means that would have ended it, but Lincoln, though he hated slavery as much as they did, wanted only to restrict it. He was "radical." Brown and Garrison were revolutionary. Lincoln meant well. Brown and Garrison were determined to do well.

But after Lincoln, even as President, had continued to temporize with slavery; after he had sent word to the Southern leaders that if they would let him write into a treaty of peace the one word "union" he would let them write all of the other words, including "slavery"—after all of this, there came a change, and Lincoln ceased to be a "radical." Then, and not until then, did he strike the blow that in his youth he declared he would strike if ever the opportunity should come. With only the briefest words he laid the Emancipation Proclamation before his cabinet.

"I do not lay this before you for your advice," he said, "but only for your information. I have promised my God that I will do this, and I shall do it."

Thus spoke the revolutionist. The time for "radicalism" had passed. Slavery, during half a century of "radicalism," had expanded. Having the power to kill chattel slavery and daring to use it, Lincoln killed chattel slavery. He put himself into the hearts of men. He wrote his name so big in history that the names of all other men since his time seem small.

Yet Lincoln, if he had been content to remain merely a "radical," could have performed no service for his country worth while, and Fame would have missed him by many a mile. If the South had won, the North would have blamed Lincoln. If the North had won, without destroying chattel slavery, nothing would have been settled, and Lincoln would have been given the credit for settling nothing. Lincoln's greatest opportunity to serve his country lay in doing precisely what he did, and it is to his eternal glory that he had both the understanding and the courage to do it.

The times again call loudly for such a man. Chattel slavery is dead, but a greater slavery has grown up in its place. Wage slavery is as much greater than chattel slavery as the white people in this country are more numerous than the black people. Poverty is widespread and the fear of poverty is all but universal. No one knows how much longer he will have employment. No one can know how much longer he will have employment. A few own all of the machinery without which we cannot be employed. These few have it in their power to say whether we shall be permitted to earn the means of life. We may want to work as much as we please, but we cannot work unless they please. They do not please to let us work unless they believe they can see a profit in so doing. That we need work means nothing to those who own the great industries of the country. Nor does the fact that the people need the things we could make. They consider only the question: "Is there profit in it?" By their answer, we eat or hunger, live or die.

Such times could not help but call for great men, even in little places. The times call for great men to take charge of municipal affairs, lest the poor shall be tortured with bad tenements and robbed of their last nickels by little grafters while greater grafters are taking their dollars. The times call for great men in state offices, in judicial positions, in Congress and in the White House. But, in response to the White House call, who answered in 1912? Mr. Roosevelt answered. Mr. Wilson answered.

Socialists do not regard either Mr. Roosevelt or Mr. Wilson as a fraudulent "radical," in the sense that they believe either of them to be intent upon wantonly fooling the people. We regard Mr. Roosevelt as being something of a self-seeker. We regard him as the embodiment of inconsistency. We know that when he was President he never tried to do some of the things that he later promised to do if we would again make him President. We know he does not now promise to try to take away the club with which robbery is committed. He is still picking at the splinters, taking care to lay no hand upon the club itself. And, so far as concerns Mr. Wilson, we regard him as an amiable, cultured gentleman, who, meaning well, as he doubtless does, lacks the understanding without which he can not do well. We also call attention to the fact that immediately following Mr. Wilson's nomination he began to placate the great grafters. He invited them to his home to hold counsel with him. And, in his speech of acceptance, he all but laid himself at their feet. He said nothing worth saying. He confined himself to platitudes. He swore allegiance to the "rule of right" as applied to government, without giving the slightest indication of his definition of right. Wall Street applauded him. Stocks went up. But would stocks have gone up if Wall Street had believed that, under Wilson, grafters would not be permitted to continue to rob you?

We Socialists may be extremely absurd persons, but, as we look about us, we see two or three things that should be done at once.

We believe every man should have the continuous right to work. We believe this right should be guaranteed by law. The law prohibits stealing and vagrancy. Why should not the law, therefore, guarantee the right to avoid the necessity for becoming either a thief or a vagrant?

We also believe that after a man has worked he should not be robbed. We believe if nobody were robbed, there would be in this country neither millionaires nor paupers. From the fact that there are in this country so many millionaires and so many paupers or near-paupers, we deduce that the extent of the robbery of the many by the few is appalling.

We want this stopped. We don't demand that it be stopped a hundred years hence—we demand that it be stopped now. We are interested in our posterity, but we are also interested in ourselves. We want to enjoy life a little. This world looks good to us. We know it could be good to us. We demand that it shall be good to us. Nor are we appeased by the promise of some "radical" like Mr. Roosevelt or Mr. Wilson that if we will elect him President, he will try to make the world a little less bad for us. The promise of a 1 per cent. or a 5 per cent. reduction in robbery constitutes no blandishment. We demand a 100 per cent. reduction in robbery. We are tired of robbery. We mean to end it. We shall end it. We cannot fail, because we have a weapon with which the robbed class never before fought. We have the gigantic printing press. Our ancestors had a puny press, or none at all. We shall carry our word far. Wherever our word goes it will wake. Sooner or later, the robbed will understand. Then robbery will cease. Millions of people who understand how to stop robbery will never consent to let a few continue to rob them.

Such is our demand—a 100 per cent. reduction in robbery and the right of the individual to continuous work. Yet, so far as we know, we want no more than is wanted by every other man who is not robbing anybody. We know of no man who is willing to be denied the right to work. We know of no man who is willing to be robbed. We differ from you Republicans and Democrats only in this: You seem to be willing to take an eternity to end robbery and secure a guarantee to the right to labor. We tell you that if you take an eternity to get these rights you will never get them. We also tell you that with either Mr. Wilson, Mr. Roosevelt or any other so-called "radical" in the White House the working class will remain poverty-stricken.

These gentlemen want to make you an omelette, but they do not want to break any eggs. They are afraid to break eggs. Breaking eggs means destroying the great fundamental laws that capitalists use to rob you. Yet, how are you ever to have an omelette unless eggs are broken? How can you be helped without hurting those who are now hurting you?

Make no mistake—anything that will make it much easier for you to live by working will make it much harder for capitalists to live without working.

Picking at the splinters of this poverty-problem will not do. The wrong is great; the remedy must be equally great.

Anything that will not hurt the capitalist class much will not help you much.

Between you and the capitalist class there can be no peace.

So long as either of you exists, there can be only war.

You will continue to fight for the right to live.

The capitalist class will continue to refuse you the right to live except at the price of a profit.

This ultimatum, which has never appealed to your stomach, will some day not appeal to your brain.

You will begin to ask questions.

You will ask if you were born only that Mr. Morgan, Mr. Armour or Mr. Ryan might be made a little richer.

You will ask if it is right that you should die when you can no longer make others richer.

Your common sense will tell you that you were not born to make anybody richer.

Your common sense will tell you that you have a right to live, whether anybody be thereby made richer.

And, when that time comes, you will be in no mood to listen to the remedies of "radical" gentlemen like Mr. Roosevelt and Mr. Wilson.

You will no longer want wage slavery "regulated"—you will want it destroyed.

You will call for another Lincoln to destroy wage slavery as the first Lincoln destroyed chattel slavery.

And your call will be answered, because you will answer it yourself.

You will place in office not only a man but *men* who will work your will. You will know what you want and you will get it, because you will know how to get it.

The reason you have never gotten what you want is because you have never known how to get it. You want the right to work without being robbed. You do not seem to realize that it is the existence of the capitalist system that causes you to be robbed. In an indefinite sort of way you seem to believe that it is possible for a small class of bondholders and share-holders to live in luxury without working and, at the same time, take nothing from the product of your labor. If dividends grew upon one tree and wages upon another, your belief would be justified. But, inasmuch as dividends and wages grow upon the same tree, your belief is not justified. Both are the products of your labor. If the bondholders were to take everything you produce, you would have nothing. If you were to take everything you produce, the bondholders and other capitalists would have nothing.

Such being the fact, what possible benefit can come to the American people through the election to the Presidency of Woodrow Wilson? Mr. Wilson is not opposed to the capitalist system. He believes one class should own all of the great industries of the country while another class toils in them. Believing thus, he necessarily believes no man has a right to work, however sore may be his need, unless some other man thinks he can see a profit in hiring him. If he did not so believe, he would not have stood for the Presidency upon the Democratic platform. The importance of securing to each individual the right to work would have prevented him from so standing. He would have proclaimed to the country an amendment to the platform in some such words as these:

"If you elect me President, I will urge the passage of a law that will make it a felony for any capitalist to refuse work at wages representing the market price of the product, except at such times as his steel plants, railroads, or other industries, are running at full capacity."

He would also have added:

"When a man's right to work is involved, I care not whether the man who hires him makes a profit or not. Life comes before profits. Work comes before life. I am for men."

Not one word of which Mr. Wilson ever said. Mr. Wilson believes in profits first and life, if at all, afterward. He may not believe he does, but he does. That is what his attitude amounts to. He wants both profits and life if we can get them. But if either must fall, it must be life. Life must always fall when work falls. Mr. Wilson stands for absolutely nothing that will put the worker's right to work before the capitalist's greed for profits. Let him or any of his friends point out a word in his platform, or any of his public utterances, to the contrary. There is no such word, because it has never been spoken or written by Mr. Wilson or anybody who is back of him or in front of him.

More astounding do these facts become as we consider them. Here is a great nation, eager to earn its bread. Of the many millions who compose this nation, not one in ten ever has or ever will receive a profit upon anything. More than nine-tenths of our many millions are wage-laborers or farmers. Naturally, they care nothing about profits. If everybody were continuously employed at good wages, and the balance-sheets, at the end of the year, should show not one dollar left for dividends, nobody except the capitalists would shed a tear. So little does the working class really care about profits.

So convinced is the working class that the right to work, together with the right to be protected from robbery, should come ahead of everything else. *Yet this very working class that cares nothing about profits; that cares and needs to care so much about the continuous right to work; that cares and needs to care so much about the right to be protected from robbery—this very working class gave Mr. Wilson almost every vote he received!*

Do the people of America know how to get what they want?

The people of America want the continuous right to work.

Mr. Wilson offers them fine phrases about the "rule of right"—phrases that Wall Street applauds because Wall Street knows such phrases mean the continued rule of wrong.

The people of America want the right to be protected from robbery, and Mr. Wilson offers them an anti-trust plank, in which they are solemnly assured that if they will only wait until Mr. Rockefeller, Mr. Morgan and other similar gentlemen are in jail, they will be very happy.

Is it not absurd? Indeed, it is not. It is pitiful. It is pitiful that a people should so long have been kept in ignorance of both the nature of their social malady and its cure. Yet, how could they be otherwise than ignorant? They depend for such information upon their newspapers, magazines, public officials, and public speakers. Until recently, almost all of these sources were poisoned against the people. They were poisoned against the people because they were controlled, in one way or another, by the capitalist class. They are still almost all poisoned in the interest of the capitalist class. The truth about Socialism is carefully suppressed. The false is carefully put forward. Wrongs are admitted, but rights are not recognized. The people are robbed, yes—but who robs them? Why, the trusts and the high-tariff gentlemen, certainly. Therefore, if we lower the tariff and place the trust gentlemen in jail, we shall be happy.

Nobody seems moved to recall whether we were happy when the tariff was low and there were no trusts.

Nobody seems to recall that the working class has never been happy; that it has always been the prey of a master class which has resorted first to one method and then to another to plunder. In fact, nobody but Socialists seems to do any serious thinking until his favorite "radical" President has passed into history without doing the slightest thing to alleviate poverty.

Grover Cleveland was regarded, each time he was elected, as radical. In Cleveland's day, not to be in favor of highway robbery in office was regarded as proof of radicalism. That is why Cleveland's dictum that "a public office is a public trust" attracted national attention. It was a new note. But in neither of Cleveland's terms did he do anything to improve the condition of the American people. They were as poor when he finally left office as they were when he first took office. Moreover, there was good reason for their poverty. Cleveland never lost an opportunity to betray them. He sold bonds in secret to Mr. Morgan to the great profit of Mr. Morgan and the great loss of the American people. He hurled troops against strikers and placed thousands of deputy United States Marshals under the orders of railway managers who were trying to prevent their employees from obtaining living wages.

Benjamin Harrison was never regarded as a radical, but in 1888 he was regarded as an improvement upon Cleveland. After Harrison had done nothing for four years, Cleveland was believed to be an improvement upon Harrison. Four years more of Cleveland were enough to send him out of office with the condemnation of everybody but the grafters in both parties.

Business revived somewhat under the Presidency of McKinley, but the revival was not so much due to anything that Mr. McKinley did as it was to the fact that the time had come for the pendulum to swing back from panic to "prosperity." Nor did the revival solve the problem of poverty. Nothing was settled because nothing was changed. Not so many men were denied the right to work, but those who worked toiled only for a "full dinner pail." They paid all they received to live poorly. Only their employers fared wonderfully well. For them there was real prosperity.

Which brings us to Mr. Roosevelt and his Progressive party.

Mr. Roosevelt was the first President of the type that is now regarded as "radical." He held office seven years and a half. He had "a perfectly corking time." He did business with all of the bosses, including Hanna, Quay, Cannon, Payne, Aldrich and a host of others, but we have his word for it that his intentions were good. Maybe they were. For the sake of argument, let it be granted that they were. Let it be conceded that he believed the things he did would enable the average man to earn a living more certainly and more easily. Still, is it not a fact that the things he did failed to accomplish what he expected they would?

Is it not a fact that it is to-day more difficult for most persons to make a living than it was when Mr. Roosevelt became President?

Is not the cost of living vastly more?

Are not more millions of men out of work?

Is there not greater uncertainty with regard to continuity of employment?

Are not more men, women and children living upon the hunger line, or close to it?

Each of these questions must be answered in the affirmative. Mr. Roosevelt, himself, would not dare, even if he were so inclined, to answer them in the negative. The facts are notorious and scandalous. They are scandalous because poverty, in this rich country, is unnecessary.

Yet, Mr. Roosevelt is not wholly to blame. He is only partly to blame. A President is not the government. He is only part of the government. As part of the government, Mr. Roosevelt advocated measures, some of which were enacted into law, that he believed would do good. Subsequent events have proved that he was in error. The measures he believed would help have not helped. If they had helped, times would be better than they were, instead of worse.

Therefore, we are brought face to face with these questions:

"If Mr. Roosevelt, during seven and one-half years in the White House, could do nothing to make the conditions of the average man's life easier, how long should we have to elect him President in order to give him time to do something worth while?

"If we were to elect him for life, are you sure that the rest of his lifetime would be long enough?

"In any event, are you prepared to wait so long to be helped?"

Mr. Roosevelt's friends, following this thought, reply that he is not the same man that he was when he left the White House; that he has grown, with vision enlarged.

No, he is not the same man. The American people have forced him into the advocacy of some things. They have forced even some Socialist measures upon him. The initiative, the referendum and the recall are Socialist measures. For a good many years, Mr. Roosevelt tried to damn them with faint praise combined with a medley of doubts and strangling provisos. But after these measures, in one winter, fought their way into every state capitol west of the Mississippi, as well as into some of the state capitols of the East, Mr. Roosevelt saw a great light. Then he became in favor of them.

When Mr. Roosevelt was President he had nothing to say against the courts. He criticised individual judges, as he criticised Judge Anderson of Indianapolis, whom he called "a damned jackass and a crook." But Judge Anderson, be it remembered, had just decided against Mr. Roosevelt in the libel suit that he brought against several newspapers because of articles reflecting upon the part played by himself and others in the acquisition of the Panama Canal property.

Now Mr. Roosevelt is convinced that our judicial system is in need of reform. In reaching this opinion, however, he is somewhat late. The courts are no longer popular. The people have not yet begun to strike at them, but they are watching them out of the corners of their eyes. Mr. Roosevelt senses the situation and responds with a proposition to give the people the right to recall, or set aside, the decisions of *state* courts. He says nothing about giving the people the right to recall the decisions of the United States Supreme Court, though he must know this court is the chief judicial offender. Yet we are asked to believe that Mr. Roosevelt, in belatedly joining the fight against the tyrannical power of the courts, is but giving proof of the greatness to which he has grown and the increased fearlessness with which he fights.

The women of the country have forced Mr. Roosevelt into the advocacy of woman suffrage. Mr. Roosevelt used to say that Mrs. Roosevelt was "only lukewarm" toward woman suffrage, and that his interest in it was the same. After the women of California gained the ballot, and Mr. Roosevelt again became a candidate for the Presidency, he changed from "lukewarm" to very hot. From that moment, woman suffrage became not only a right, but a necessity. Of course, the fact that women vote in several western states that he hoped to carry had no part whatever in changing his opinion. Mr. Roosevelt is not that kind of a man.

Mr. Roosevelt's 1912 platform—or "contract with the people," as he calls it—bristles with new devices and new plans for the public good. Some of Mr. Roosevelt's plans would probably help a little—provided he could get a Congress that would put them into effect, and courts that would declare them constitutional. Mr. Lincoln probably could have helped the black slaves a little if he had made it a legal obligation upon slave owners to provide each negro, semi-annually, with a red necktie and a paste diamond. Mr. Lincoln might have gone even further and provided that each negro should be supplied, during the water-melon season, with all the melons he could eat. Instead, he wrote the Emancipation Proclamation.

Mr. Roosevelt's present political program is by no means an emancipation proclamation to the American people. It unties no knots, nor cuts any. It bristles with Socialists' phrases, but it does not bristle with Socialist remedies. "This country belongs to the people who inhabit it"—an assertion that appears in Mr. Roosevelt's platform—is a Socialist phrase. But Mr. Roosevelt's method of giving the people their own is not Socialistic. The Socialist method is to give it to them. Mr. Roosevelt's method is to appoint "strong" commissions to regulate the country that the people own, but do not control or enjoy. Again and again in his platform Mr. Roosevelt fervently advocates a "strong" commission to do this or do that.

If the word "strong" in a platform were sufficient to make a commission "strong" in action we might expect the commissions that Mr. Roosevelt advocates to be as strong as any commission can be that is trying to regulate other people's property.

But we do not believe the word "strong" in a platform makes a commission strong. Mr. Roosevelt, always preaching strenuosity, nevertheless appointed, during his Presidency, some exceedingly poor officials.

Since Mr. Roosevelt, the originator of "strong" commissions as a cure for the poverty that is produced by robbery, failed as he did, what should we expect from such commissions if they were appointed by Presidents of the ordinary Wall Street stripe?

Simmered down, Mr. Roosevelt's Progressive Party stands simply for this: We are still to have trusts and tariffs, but only such trusts and tariffs as Mr. Roosevelt wants. We are still to have a master class who own all of the industries and a servant class who do all of the work, but masters and servants must conduct themselves as Mr. Roosevelt provides. Masters may still hold out for profits and servants may die for lack of opportunity to work, but so long as Mr. Roosevelt, at Armageddon, is "fighting for the Lord," what of it?

Such is not Mr. Roosevelt's reasoning, but it might as well be. Mr. Roosevelt and Mr. Wilson, like all other "radical" politicians, are incapable of rendering any great service to the American people for the simple reason that they do not strike at the great wrong. The great wrong is the ownership, by a small class, of the great class's means of life. A people who cannot support themselves without asking the permission of others are little more than slaves. We are such a people.

"Radicals" who promise, if given power, to free us, only mock us. Such gentlemen are not radicals at all. The word "radical" is derived from a Greek word meaning "root." A real radical is one who goes to the roots of things. But radicals like Mr. Roosevelt and Mr. Wilson go to the roots of nothing.

The only way to go to the root of anything is to go to it.

Lincoln went to the root of the chattel slavery question.

When he had finished, the chattel slavery question was no longer a question—it was a corpse. After wasting years of his life as an anti-slavery "radical" he became an anti-slavery revolutionist and destroyed slavery. Lincoln, during the last two years of his life, became a real radical. A real radical and a revolutionist are but different names for the same thing.

The working class is suffering from robbery. The working class has always suffered from robbery. Never has there been a time when a little crowd of grafters were not feeding upon the workers.

In the beginning, the working class were held as chattel slaves, the only possible cure for which was the utter destruction of chattel slavery.

Then the workers became the serfs of feudal lords, the only possible cure for which was the destruction of feudalism.

Now the toilers are robbed by the private ownership of the means of production, the only possible cure for which is the destruction of such ownership and the substitution of public ownership through the agency of government.

No tinkering will do. Tinkering could not and did not settle the white man's or the black man's slavery question. Nothing but the absolute destruction of the capitalist system can remove the poverty, the ignorance, the crime and the vice that are inevitable products of the system.

But do not expect capitalists to remove this system for you. They will not.

You never saw a tiger feed its prey. You never saw a burglar mend a victim's roof. You may see both of these sights some day. If you should, you may, perhaps, prepare yourself to behold the more marvelous spectacle of the capitalist class financing the campaign of a genuine radical who is bent upon taking the capitalist class off your back.

But until you see a tiger feeding its prey, you may well ask yourself whether "radicals" whose campaigns are financed by great capitalists are radical enough to do you any good.

Certainly one side or the other is always doomed to disappointment; either the capitalists who put up the money or the workers who put up the votes. The capitalists are still doing quite well. Are you?

CHAPTER IX
THE TRUTH ABOUT THE COAL QUESTION

Almost anyone can make anybody believe anything that is not so. It is only the truth that makes poor headway in this world. Our national motto seems to be: "When there are no more blunderers or liars to be heard, let us listen to common sense."

The anthracite coal situation is a case in point. So long ago as 1902 this situation had become maddening. As the result of a prolonged strike to obtain living wages for the miners, the country, at the beginning of winter, was threatened with a coal famine. So serious was the situation that a "Get-Coal Conference" was held at Detroit. Among the delegates were Victor L. Berger, the first Socialist congressman, and a number of other Socialists. These Socialist delegates told the conference what to do. They said:

"Go into politics. Make the governmental ownership of the coal mines and the railroads a political matter. Take over the ownership of these mines and railroads and operate them for the benefit of the people, rather than for the benefit of millionaires. Do that and you will have solved your coal problem."

But that was the truth, mind you. As truth, it had no chance of acceptance at that time. Truth never has a chance the first time, the second time or the third time. Truth has attained its great reputation for rising every time it is crushed only because it has been so often crushed.

And the truth that these men spoke in Detroit years ago was forthwith crushed, not only in Detroit, but all over the country. What was the use of believing? Were there not plenty of blunderers about? Were there not plenty of blind alleys in which to go?

Indeed, there were. The people went into one of them. Or, rather, they remained in the blind alley in which they had long been. That was the blind alley of private ownership of the coal mines and railroads. Plenty of blind men could see a delightful opening at the end of this blind alley. They were very sure that it led somewhere. It must lead somewhere. Certainly, no great difficulty could be encountered in managing these millionaires. The Inter-State Commerce Commission would fix them if nothing else could fix them. If the Inter-State Commerce Commission should prove too weak for the task, the courts would not prove too weak. At any rate, there was no danger ahead. It was entirely safe to leave the nation's coal supply in the hands of a few men who had already abundantly proved their disinclination to treat either their employees or the public honestly.

For ten straight years thereafter we fought the Coal Trust in the courts. We enjoined it, we indicted it, we prosecuted it. To what purpose? To no purpose. In 1912, the United States Supreme Court brought an end to the proceedings by handing down a decision that was said to be a "great victory" for the Government. But it was one of those great anti-trust victories that do not hurt the trusts nor help the people. This "victory" did not hurt the Coal Trust. The price of coal did not go down a nickel. On the contrary, the prices of coal road stocks immediately went higher. Wall Street knew the decision would not interrupt the Coal Trust in its plundering, and backed its opinion with its money. Wall Street quickly realized what we have not yet fully realized—that the court had prohibited only a certain method of stealing, while leaving the trust free to adopt any one of a hundred other methods, each of which is as suitable to its purposes as the method that has been put under the ban.

The trust lawyers quickly juggled out one of the hundred other methods of stealing and the robbery of the people continued as if there had been no decision by the United States Supreme Court. Immediately, there was a loud demand from the "radical" press that the anti-trust law be so amended that it would prohibit the new form of robbery. Again the Socialists repeated their warning against reliance upon laws that seek to regulate trusts. Again the Socialists urged the people to settle the coal question for all time by owning and operating the coal mines and the railroads that carry the coal to the people. Between the advice given by Socialists and the advice given by radicals, there was all the difference that there is between night and day. The "radicals" advised the people to leave the coal in the hands of a few multi-millionaires and then fight in the courts to get it back. The Socialists assured the people that if they would take possession of their own coal they would not be compelled to fight to get it back. But the advice given by the Socialists contained too much truth to find ready acceptance. There being not fewer than a hundred ways in which the trust could rob the people, it seemed so much more reasonable to let the trust try these various ways, one by one, and prosecute the trust gentlemen for each separate form of robbery. Ten years were required to "win" the anti-trust case that was finally decided in 1912, so we shall require at least 1,000 years to obtain supreme court decisions prohibiting a hundred different methods of Coal Trust robbery. But good, able "radical" gentlemen assured the people that the way to kill the Coal Trust was to choke it with court decisions and the people believed what they were told. Almost always the people believe what they are told unless what they are told is true. It is only the truth that must fight its way in this world. So many powerful, selfish persons are always eager to foist the lie that feathers their nests. Truth is always besmirched by those whom it would destroy, and too often despised by those whom it would help.

Thus we have a naked view of two classes of men—the anthracite coal operators and their victims. The coal operators are conscienceless robbers.

They hold within the hollows of their hands the anthracite coal supply of this country. They own it or control it as you own or control a gas range that you have bought or rented. The coal supply of this country is their property. And though you must draw upon it or freeze in winter, you cannot have a pound of coal except at their price. And their price is always all they believe they can get out of you without a riot. The cost of production does not matter. Your necessities do not matter. They want all they can get.

These naked millionaires are not attractive persons. Who would be an attractive person if he had their power? Are you so sure you would be an attractive person if you had their power? Do not be too sure. Give any man such an opportunity to squeeze millions out of a people and it is very likely that he will squeeze them. There is little or nothing in this "good man," "bad man" theory. The blackest Coal Trust magnate is just what you and the Coal Trust have made him. If anything, you are more to blame than he. He gets all of his power from the laws. And the men whom you elect make the laws. They make the laws which say that a few men—or, so far as that is concerned, one man—may own all of the anthracite coal mines in the country.

These laws are certainly very comfortable for the Coal Trust gentlemen. If you are satisfied, they are. If you don't move to change them, they will never move to change them. But, if you are fit to cast a ballot, you know that the present conditions can never be changed until the laws that made the conditions are changed.

Let us now take a close view of the Coal Trust victims. You are one of them. You are tired of the Coal Trust. You have no sort of notion that it is anything except the robber concern that everybody believes it to be. You would be much better pleased if the government owned the mines. You would be still better pleased if the government owned not only the mines but the railroads that carry coal from the mines. You know that in the Panama Canal Zone, where the government sells all of the supplies, the cost of living is much less than it is here. You believe all of this and more. But what are you doing to translate your belief into accomplished fact?

You are doing nothing. The only way in which you can translate this belief into accomplished fact is to express your belief in political action. You must vote for that which you believe. You must support a political party that advocates the ownership by the government of the coal mines and the railroads. If you vote for a party that believes in permitting the ownership of the coal mines and the railroads to remain where it is you are voting for the Coal Trust. How long do you believe it will take you to beat the Coal Trust by voting for the Coal Trust? Do you know of any way in which the Coal Trust can be beaten except by voting against it?

Of course, the newspapers that you read will tell you there are other ways of beating the robber Coal Trust than by voting against it. They will tell you that the Coal Trust can be "regulated" or indicted and convicted into decency. Ask your newspapers what makes them think so. We have many great trusts in this country—has a single one of them ever been regulated into decency? Have they been so ruthlessly pursued in court that they were willing to be decent? You know the answer. You know there is not a decent great trust in the country. You know that every attempt to drive them into decency has failed. Yet your newspapers have the impudence to tell you that it is not necessary that the government should own the anthracite mines and the railroads.

It would be difficult to imagine a more amazing situation. Here we have in this country two sharply contrasted classes of opinion.

One opinion is that institutions like the Coal Trust should be regulated or destroyed—compelled to go back to competition.

The other opinion is that institutions like the Coal Trust can neither be regulated nor compelled to break up into small parts and compete.

The men who hold the first opinion can not point to a single instance wherein their belief has been justified by events. The men who hold the second opinion have only common sense with which to back up their assertion that, if the government owned the coal mines and the railroads, Coal Trust magnates and railway multi-millionaires could not rob us.

But in this instance, as in all others where the robbery of the many by the few is concerned, truth is put upon the defensive. The grafters, as they might naturally be expected to do, not only shower upon the truth-tellers their scorn and derision, but even the people who are being robbed are doubtful or suspicious. They are not so certain that if robbers be stopped robbery will be stopped. They suspect the statement that, if nothing be taken from something, something will remain untouched. They want us to prove, not only that two and two make four, but that nothing from four leaves four.

But they don't ask the "regulation" send-them-to-jail gentlemen to prove anything. When these grafters say two from four leave four nobody expresses a doubt. Everybody is ready to believe that that which has never been done can be easily done. Few are ready to believe that that which might easily be done can be done at all.

The public attitude toward the Coal Trust and the railroads constitutes possibly the only exception to this rule. The Coal Trust and the railroads have so wronged the people that the people would doubtless welcome their ownership by the government. If the people were to vote directly upon the question: "Shall the government take over the ownership of the anthracite coal mines and the railroads?" it is probable that the affirmative majority would be not less than two to one. Yet, notwithstanding the fact that the coal question can be solved only with ballots, the Socialists are the only ones who seem ever to try with their ballots to solve it. The rest of the people, while opposed to the conditions that exist, vote the tickets of parties that are pledged to maintain the conditions that exist.

Every man who voted for Wilson, Roosevelt or Taft voted to keep the coal supply of the nation in private hands and the railroads in private hands.

Those who voted for Mr. Wilson voted to "destroy" the Coal Trust and "send the trust magnates to prison."

Those who voted for Mr. Roosevelt voted to permit the Coal Trust to continue to own the nation's coal supply, provided only that it be "good." Otherwise, a "strong" commission appointed by Mr. Roosevelt would proceed to administer "social justice."

Those who voted for Mr. Taft voted to break the Coal Trust into bits.

Candidly, let us ask, did either of these plans suit anybody? Is there anybody who would not have vastly preferred that the government take over the ownership of the anthracite coal mines and operate them for the benefit of the people? A plan of governmental ownership and operation would have settled the coal question instantly. A government that can dig the Panama Canal can dig coal.

But there is no likelihood whatever that Mr. Wilson's plan to destroy the Coal Trust and all other trusts will settle the coal question at all. The Coal Trust cares nothing for courts. Mr. Hearst attacked the Coal Trust more vigorously in the courts than any President ever attacked any trusts in the courts. Mr. Hearst came out of court absolutely empty-handed. He gained a few paper victories, but he gained no substantial victory. He never halted for a moment the upward flight of the price of coal.

Mr. Wilson, if he try ever so hard, can do no better. So long as the principle of the private ownership of the anthracite coal fields is admitted—and Mr. Wilson admits this principle as fully as does anybody—nothing can be done. Corporations can be split up into bits, it is true, as the Standard Oil Company was split up, but what do such splits amount to? Absolutely nothing. The ownership is not changed. The dominating owners continue to handle the pieces as they formerly handled the whole.

Suppose Mr. Wilson try to enforce the criminal clause of the Sherman Anti-Trust law and put the coal magnates into jail? Suppose he try to compel the component parts of the Coal Trust actually to compete with each other. What will happen?

This will happen. The component parts of the Coal Trust will refuse to compete. The men who are at the head of the coal companies are business associates of long standing. They know each other well, and they know well that none of them can make any money by fighting any of the others. So, when one gentleman announces a schedule of coal prices, none of the others will undercut him. All of the other coal companies will announce the same prices, because the owners of each company will also be the owners of all the other companies.

Did you ever stop to consider what position the government will then be in? Will not its hands be tied? Can the government go into court and demand that the other companies cut their prices? Suppose the other companies say they cannot cut their prices without losing money? Suppose the other companies say nothing at all, except: "This coal belongs to us. We have quite as much right to fix our own price upon it as has the government to fix its own price upon postage stamps. That other coal companies have fixed the same price we have is no more the government's business than it is because several grocers fix the same price upon sugar, bacon, tea or coffee."

It will then be up to the government to prove that the identicality of prices is the result of conspiracy. If conspiracy cannot be proved, the government can do nothing. In such a case, the government would never be able to prove conspiracy. The coal operators would not conspire over the telephone, or on the street corners. There would be little for them to conspire about, anyway. All of them would be financially interested in all of the companies, precisely as Mr. Rockefeller is financially interested in all of the constituent companies of the Standard Oil Company. The matter of price-fixing would probably be left to the dominating personality of the group, precisely as it is now left, more or less, to the strongest man among them. And, the prices he fixed would speedily become the prices of all.

Thus do we perceive a peculiar feature of the human mind. Individually, we know what we should like to do about the Coal Trust and the railroads. We know we should like to own and operate them. But collectively we know no such thing. We do not get together. We act as if that which each of us believes were believed by no other than himself. We are like butter that will not "gather" or bees that will not "hive."

There is every reason why we who are paying outrageous prices for coal should get together on the matter of public ownership. The cost of mining coal is less than $2 a ton. In 1902 Mr. George F. Baer—the "Divine Right" gentleman—testified that the cost was $2, and some other witnesses testified that it was as low as $1.43 a ton. Probably no one but the coal magnates know exactly what the cost is, but now and then a fact leaks out that is illuminating.

Such a fact was discovered in 1912 by a staff correspondent whom the New York *World* sent into the coal regions.

The *World* man found that the Coal Trust sells coal to its employees at a reduced price. This is not philanthropy, because if the Coal Trust charged full price for coal, it would soon be compelled to pay the miners more wages—they live like dogs, and not much more can be taken from them until it is first given to them. At any rate, the *World* man found that the price of coal, to miners, is only $2 a ton.

Now, it is fair to assume that the Coal Trust is not losing any money on the $2 coal that it is selling to its employees. It is more likely that it is making a nickel or two. At any rate, $2 a ton may be considered the extreme limit of the cost of mining a ton of anthracite.

Whenever the people of this country are ready to listen to the truth about the coal question, the retail price of coal can quickly be more than cut in two. The actual cost of mining coal and transporting it to any point within 500 miles of the mines probably is not more than $3 a ton. If the people, through the government, owned and operated the mines, the government could afford to sell coal at this price, plus the local cost of delivery. The wages of the miners could be doubled—as they should be—and coal could still be sold by the government at $5 a ton. In any calculation about the coal problem, the miners should not be forgotten. The Coal Trust will never take care of them, but they have a right to demand that they shall be taken care of.

The business of mining coal is dangerous and disagreeable to the last degree. Coal miners, when they are at work, seldom see the day. They go from the night of the surface to the night of the mines. They breathe such dust as never blew in the filthiest street. When a fall of slate comes or an explosion of firedamp, their mangled bodies are all that is left for their weeping widows and orphans at the mouth of the mine. If they escape death by accident, they cannot escape the death that comes from the unhealthfulness of their calling. No life insurance company wants much to do with a coal miner except at the highest rates. No tuberculosis exhibit is complete without the blackened lungs of a coal miner in a jar of alcohol. There is nothing for a coal miner when he is alive but a cheerless existence of the greatest drudgery—and nothing for him when he is dead but an unmarked grave on the hillside. Yet 76,000 human beings thus spend their lives in the anthracite coal mines, and hundreds of other thousands in the bituminous mines. All of this great toll of human misery that the nation may burn coal.

If the nation could not get along without coal, there might be some excuse for this colossal sacrifice. Even then, it would be hard for those who might be compelled to make the sacrifice and, if we were to be fair about it, we might have some difficulty in determining who should go to the mines and who should go to the opera. If we were to be fair about it, perhaps some of those who now go to the opera would go to the mines sometimes. But the nation could easily get along without sending anybody into the mines. Water power and fuel oil will do everything that coal is now doing.

Please consider the water power question. In a report made to President Taft in 1912 by Commissioner of Corporations Herbert K. Smith, these statements appear:

Steam and gas engines are creating in this country approximately 19,000,000 horsepower.

Water wheels, in this country, are developing 6,000,000 horsepower.

The water power of this country, capable of development, is approximately 19,000,000 horsepower.

These statements mean that there is enough undeveloped water power in this country to more than take the place of every coal-burning steam engine. This water power, if converted into electricity, would do everything that steam does and more. It would run machinery. It would light streets. It would heat houses. Moreover, the water power, once developed, would not have to be dug out of the ground every year. "White coal," as the Italians call water power, is mined by the sun and thrown into the furnace by the force of gravitation. Railroads need not haul it. Nobody need deliver it. It hauls and delivers itself.

But that is not all. If there were not an ounce of water power in this country, still we should not be dependent upon coal for heat and power. Oil will burn quite as well as coal—in fact, a good deal better. Dr. Rudolph Diesel, of Munich, in 1912 declared before the Institute of Mechanical Engineers in London that exhaustive researches had indicated the presence of as much oil in the globe as there is coal; that new oil fields were constantly being discovered, Borneo, Mexico and even Egypt, in addition to other known lands, containing great fields; that "the world's production of crude oil had increased three and a half times as rapidly as the production of coal, and that the ratio of increase was becoming steadily greater."

Why then do we continue to burn coal? For the same reason that we continue to do a number of other foolish things. Because we do not manage this country in which we live. The men who are managing it are managing it for profit. If there were a greater profit for the Coal Trust in switching from coal to water power or oil they would switch us quickly enough. If we were to change to oil, it would be a simple matter to lay oil pipes in the streets precisely as we now lay water and gas pipes, and heat our houses with oil sprays blown into our furnaces with jets of steam. Certainly, there would be no difficulty in heating houses from a central heating plant that burned oil.

Plenty of western cities have such central heating plants now that burn coal. And the idea is a good one, too. The central plant decreases the danger of fire, besides doing away with dust and the necessity of shoveling coal into the furnace of each house.

But gentlemen like the Coal Trust barons figure this way: "We have a certain amount of money invested here. We are looking only for the highest rate of interest that we can get upon our investment. We might serve the people better if we were to turn to water power development or the burning of oil, but it is doubtful if we should obtain a greater rate of interest upon our investment. Certainly, we should lose a lot by junking our coal mines, as we should be compelled to do if we were to prove their worthlessness—so, we'll just keep on dealing in coal."

And, the people of the United States, through their failure to "get together" politically behind some party that stands for what they all want—the people of the United States are getting the worst of it.

If the people of the United States want their government—which is actually themselves, though they do not seem to know it—if the people of the United States want their government to take over and to operate the coal mines solely for the benefit of the people of the United States, they can do it simply by standing together and talking and voting for what they want.

In the meantime, it would be a splendid thing for the country if the Coal Trust would increase the price of coal a dollar a month until such time as the people become enough interested in their own problems to solve them.

CHAPTER X
DEATHBEDS AND DIVIDENDS

Stock market reports do not show a relationship between deathbeds and dividends. Such a relationship exists, however. In this country, many are made to die miserably in order that a few may live magnificently. Every year, more than half a million human beings are compelled to die in order that a few thousands may make, every year, perhaps half a billion dollars. More than three millions are kept sick in order that a handful may be kept rich.

This is not mere rhetoric. It is fact. Irving Fisher, Professor of Political Economy at Yale, and President of the Committee of One Hundred on National Health, is one of the authorities for the figures. In his report on national vitality, to the Conservation Commission, he declared that in this country, every year, 600,000 human beings die whose lives might be saved; that there are constantly 3,000,000 ill who might be well.

Dr. Woods Hutchinson, New York physician, endorses these estimates. Moreover, the estimates are confirmed by the actual experience of New Zealand. New Zealand's death-rate is 9.5 to the thousand. Our death-rate is 16.5 to the thousand. If New Zealand's population were as great as our own, the number of deaths each year, under her present rate, would be 630,000 fewer than the number of Americans who die each year. Yet the climate of New Zealand is no more healthful than is that of America. New Zealand simply does not sacrifice her people to private greed. America does.

Plenty of laymen know how typhoid could be made a dead disease. Germany has already made typhoid all but a dead disease in Germany. Yet, in this country, tuberculosis, typhoid and other diseases that could easily be prevented, are permitted to go on, killing their millions.

Why? Because capitalism stands in the way. Because deathbeds could not be decreased in number without decreasing dividends in size. Because we can reduce the death-rate only by acting through our governments—national, state and municipal—and big business, rather than ourselves, controls these governments. Big business, desiring to keep the special privileges it has and to get more, puts men into office whom it believes will do its bidding. Usually, these men know nothing and care nothing about promoting the public health. They are politicians. If they do know something about promoting the public health, and attempt to apply their knowledge at the expense of somebody's dividends, there is a fight. If it is a disease-infected tenement that it is desired to tear down, the injunction is brought into play.

Such a situation seems appalling. It is appalling. It borders upon the monstrous that a people who have at last learned how to prevent the great diseases should not be permitted to apply their knowledge. That the people endure such a condition can be explained only on the theory that they realize neither the ease with which modern science could extend their lives, nor the identity of the few who put dividends above life.

In order that there shall be no doubt concerning the power of present knowledge, if applied, to destroy some of the great diseases and cripple others, I shall set down here a question that I asked of Professor Irving Fisher, Dr. Woods Hutchinson, and Dr. J. N. McCormack. Dr. McCormack is an eminent physician, who devotes his entire time to lecturing throughout the United States, under the auspices of the American Medical Association and the Committee of One Hundred. His topic is the advisability of applying modern knowledge to the public health problem. Here is the question:

"If you had the power of a czar, could you destroy tuberculosis and typhoid fever, and also greatly reduce the number of deaths from pneumonia?"

Professor Fisher and Dr. McCormack replied promptly in the affirmative. Evidently, I might as well have asked Dr. Hutchinson if, having a glass of water, he could drink it. He was most matter of fact. Without a doubt, tuberculosis could be destroyed. So could typhoid fever, which is solely a filth disease that no one can get without eating or drinking matter that has passed through the stomach of a typhoid victim. Parenthetically, I may say that I heard Dr. Hutchinson tell a committee of the United States Senate that if a National Department of Health were established and properly administered, half of the crime would cease in twenty-five years. Dr. Hutchinson also said that it was entirely possible to save the babies that died from preventable diseases—dysentery, for instance. The lowest estimate of the number of babies who die every year from preventable diseases is 100,000.

Ask the same question of any physician in the country who is worth his salt and he will give the same answer. Thus well known are the methods by which the great diseases might be destroyed.

The way to wipe out tuberculosis quickly, for instance, would be to destroy every habitation that is known to be hopelessly infected—and there are many such—permit no habitation to be erected without provision for sufficient sunlight and air; permit no factory or other workplace to be erected without sufficient provision for sunlight and fresh air—and destroy such workplaces as now exist without this provision; reduce the cost of living so that the millions who now cannot afford to live in sanitary homes and buy adequate food could do so; isolate the infected and educate the people with regard to the necessity of sleeping with their bedroom windows wide open.

If this program were put through, tuberculosis would cease as soon as those who are now infected should either have recovered or died. It is because such a program has not been put through that, according to Professor Fisher, there are always 500,000 Americans suffering from tuberculosis, and the annual death-roll from the disease is 150,000. Any municipal government, if it were disposed to do so and the courts were willing to let it do so, could put through the housing part of the program in a single summer. The dangerous habitations could be condemned. The government, if necessary, could build and rent at cost, sanitary houses in the suburbs, as the government of New Zealand does for its people. Congress, the President and the courts, if they were disposed to do so, could reduce the cost of living. If the government can teach farmers by mail how to prevent hog-cholera, there would seem to be no reason why it should not teach human beings by mail to breathe fresh air both night and day.

What stands in the way of immediately putting through such a program? Nothing in the world except the men whose property would be destroyed, or whose stealings in food-prices would be stopped. The property loss would be enormous. (Think of calling the destruction of a lot of death-traps a "loss.") The "value" of the property destroyed might be a billion dollars. Maybe it would be two billions. What difference need it make if it should take five billion dollars' worth of labor, lumber, bricks, steel and other materials to replace death-traps with life-traps? One hundred and fifty thousand lives would be saved every year from tuberculosis alone, and the rebuilding operations would create greater prosperity for labor than was ever created by any act of Congress.

A hundred years ago, no one knew how to stamp out tuberculosis. What good does it do us to know how? We are not permitted to apply our knowledge. We can peck away if we want to, at the edge of the problem, but we mustn't strike at the middle. If we should, we might cut somebody's dividends. We might interfere with the "vested interests" of the owners of the cellars in which 25,000 New York families live, or with the owners of the 101,000 windowless rooms in which New Yorkers live, or with the owners of the unsanitary houses and factories in other cities. Our public officials know better than to try to do anything really radical in the health line. They have condemned just enough pestholes to know how dangerous it is to political prospects to grapple with property, and enforced just enough of the factory laws to know how dangerous it is to try to enforce factory laws at all.

In New York City, according to Tenement House Commissioner Murphy, 45 persons are burned alive every year in death-trap tenements. A new tenement house law prohibits the erection of death-traps, and in the new tenements there are no cremations. But the old death-traps are permitted to stand. In ten years, 450 more persons will have been burned alive. In 10 years, 1,500,000 more Americans will have died from tuberculosis.

"Of the people living in the United States to-day," said J. Pease Norton, Assistant Professor of Political Economy at Yale, "more than 8,000,000 will die of tuberculosis." Between the ages of 20 and 30, every third death is from consumption, and, at all ages, the mortality from the same disease is one in nine.

We now censure ancient kings for having slaughtered men in war for private profit. But what ancient king ever made such a record in war as our dividend-takers make in peace? What ancient king, in his whole lifetime, ever slew 8,000,000 men? What modern war marked the end of so many men as tuberculosis kills in a year? During the four years of the Civil War, only a little more than 200,000 men were killed in battle. Tuberculosis kills 300,000 Americans every two years. Other diseases that could be prevented if dividends were out of the way bring up the total of avoidable deaths in this country to 1,200,000 every two years.

What if our Government did nothing to end a war that was killing 600,000 Americans each year? What if a few contractors who were making millions out of the war controlled elections, administrations and the courts and would not let the government end the war?

What difference does it make whether foreign foes and army contractors kill these millions, or whether domestic dividend-takers and their governments kill them? Dead men not only "tell no tales," but they have no preferences. It is as bad to be dead from one cause as from another.

"During the next ten years," said Professor Norton, "more than 6,000,000 infants less than two years old will end their little spans of life, while mothers sit by and watch in utter helplessness. And yet this number could probably be decreased by as much as half. But nothing is done."

Dr. Cressey L. Wilbur, Chief Statistician for Vital Statistics for the Federal Census Bureau, says that at least 100,000 and perhaps 200,000 children less than five years old die in this country every year from preventable causes.

Our national government freights the mails with circulars telling how to cure hog-cholera and kill the insects that prey on fruit trees; but in all the years since the Revolutionary War, it has never sent a circular to a mother telling her how to keep her baby alive. The state and the municipal governments have done something, but they have usually stopped when they reached the big money bags. Not a state or a city has made it impossible for a baby to be given bad milk. Not a state or a city has rid itself of unsanitary habitations.

Not a state or a city has condemned all the workshops in which men and women work at the peril of their lives. Not a state or a city has even enforced its own factory-inspection laws.

If the men whom big business has put in office were even intelligently interested in public health, probably 50,000 babies could be saved each year without tearing down a rookery or providing a single better house. A little intelligent effort and a few thousand dollars would suffice.

Dr. Hutchinson tells what a little intelligent effort and a few dollars did for the babies of the small English city of Huddersfield. A few years ago a physician was elected mayor. One of his first acts was to announce that he would give a prize of ten shillings to the mother of every child born during the mayor's administration, provided the babies were brought to his office in perfect health, on the first anniversary of their birth. The only other stipulation was that no mother should be eligible to a prize who did not immediately report to the mayor the birth of her infant.

Though the prize was small, there was no lack of mothers who were willing to be takers. The doctor-mayor established what amounted to a correspondence school for mothers, and, at the birth of each child, began to send circulars telling how to take care of the baby; what to feed it and what not to feed it; what to do if the baby appeared so-and-so—and so on. Moreover, he kept a city physician on the circuit to look in at each home as often as possible, to see how the babies appeared and give the mothers further advice.

That's all there is to this story—except that he brought down the death-rate for babies from 130 to 55; saved 75 babies each year to each thousand born. More than that he helped the babies who would have lived anyway. Good care, says the doctor, will increase the strength of strong babies from 15 to 25 per cent.

Any American government could do as much. By condemning unsanitary homes any American government could do more. All that is necessary is the desire—and the permission of those who control the governments. The people that cast the ballots are willing to give the permission, but the ballots they cast perpetuate the conditions against which they complain. Otherwise, there would be no death-trap houses; nor impure food; nor extortionate food-prices; nor unsanitary workplaces. And somebody would go to jail if an ice trust, desiring to cripple competitors who might cut prices, should send ships up a river to destroy the ice. It was brought out in court that the New York Ice Trust did that. The ice trust was convicted under the State anti-trust law. But nobody is in jail. And ice is still selling at a price that kills the children of the poor.

The only way to get big business on the side of public health is to get public health and private profit on the same side. Health makes efficiency, efficiency makes profit, and whenever public health can be bought at a price that seems likely to yield a profit in efficiency, big business will buy. That is the way Professor Fisher figures it out and here is a case that he cites in point:

The girls in one of the Chicago telephone exchanges that is located in a particularly smoky and dusty part of the city complained to the manager of the smoke and dust. He cheerfully advised them to forget the smoke and dust and go on with their work, which, having more hunger than money, they did.

A few months later a growing volume of complaints against bad service caused the manager to investigate. He found that the smoke and dust were interfering with the operation of the switchboards. The little brass tags were so gummed that frequently they did not fall when subscribers called. Nor did the grime on the "plugs" with which connections are made constitute a good medium for the flow of electricity.

When the manager learned what the smoke and dust were doing to his human machines he did nothing. But when he learned what smoke and dust were doing to his metallic machines he wasted no time. He laid the matter before his superiors, with the result that a plan was installed for the filtration, through water, of every particle of air that entered the exchange.

It is not to the interest of big business as a whole that the people should have pure food. The markets are flooded with unwholesome food that an honest law, honestly administered, would have barred. Professor Fisher relates an incident that shows how afraid the big meat dealers are of the pure food law.

The professor was sitting in the lobby of a hotel not distant from New York. The proprietor of the hotel called up a New York meat dealer on the long-distance 'phone to complain that some bad beef had been sent to the hotel. He said he had never yet fed his patrons on rotten beef and he didn't intend to begin. The beef must be taken away and the charge deducted from his bill. The man at the other end of the wire evidently offered no opposition, and the receiver was hung up.

Soon the telephone rang again. New York was on the wire. The conversation was brief. All that Professor Fisher could hear was the hotel man's single remark: "I'll see what I can do and let you know."

The hotel man rang off and immediately called up a local restaurant. Then Professor Fisher heard this cheerful statement go over the wire:

"I've got some beef here that ain't just right, and the New York people who sent it to me wanted me to see if I couldn't sell it for them up here ... Oh, it'll hang together yet, but 'tain't what I want for my people; you might use it, though ... I don't know what the price will be. You'll have to make your bargain with them, but it won't be much.... All right, send over and get it."

And this—and a thousand times more than this—under the Pure Food Law! Such crimes could not occur if the government, when it tried to enact a decent law, had not been thrown flat on its back. The pity of it is that when big business and a government come into collision over public health matters, the government is usually thrown on its back.

"I doubt," said Dr. Hutchinson, "whether there is a local health officer at any post of entry in the United States who, if a case of plague, cholera or yellow fever should appear on a ship, would not think three or four times before he reported it. And if he did report it, as the law requires him to do, his act would cost him his position. Business interests would cause his removal."

This is not mere talk. Nor is it simply prophecy. It is history. So long as New Orleans was subject to periodical outbreaks of yellow fever, the health authorities were compelled not only to fight the disease, but to fight the business interests that denied its existence. Dr. Hutchinson says that business interests once caused the removal of the State health officer of Louisiana, merely because he insisted that yellow fever existed in the State—which it did.

Dr. Hutchinson himself, as State health officer of Oregon, in 1905–6, had to fight big business to conserve public health. Big business whipped him. His experiences were not novel, but one of them will be related for the simple reason that it was not novel, and therefore shows the sort of opposition that health officers, all over the land, are compelled to encounter.

Soon after taking office Dr. Hutchinson began an investigation of the water supplies of the chief cities of Oregon. His report showed that the water that private corporations were serving to municipalities carried typhoid infection.

Immediately the business interests of the State turned their guns upon him. Through the newspapers, which they controlled by reason of advertising contracts, they denounced him as an "enemy of the State." "The fair fame of the commonwealth" was being traduced by a reckless maligner. He was even dared to show his face in one city. An attempt was made to remove him from office, but the governor happened to be a man who could not be browbeaten, and Dr. Hutchinson remained.

But while the business interests of Oregon were not able to get the governor, they got somebody. The city officials who could have purified the water took no step to do so. If they had merely recognized the existence of infected water and urged the people to boil it, some service would have been performed. But the municipal officials upheld the "fair fame" of their various communities by denying that the water was infected. Notwithstanding their denials typhoid soon broke out. The outbreak at Eugene, the seat of the State university, was particularly severe. Several students died.

Yet the San Francisco plague case must long stand as the classic illustration of the manner in which business fights government when a great disease comes. Black plague—the deadliest known to the Orient; a disease that, more than once, has killed 5,000,000 persons during a single outbreak—appeared in San Francisco in 1900. The local board of health quarantined the Chinese district, and the news went out over the country. The horror of horrors had arrived! The black plague! It sent a shudder over the land.

It sent a greater shudder over the business interests of San Francisco. These business interests quickly saw visions of quarantines against the State and cessation of tourist traffic. An appeal was made to a Federal Judge to declare the quarantine illegal. He promptly did so. In giving his decision, he went out of his way to make this statement:

"If it were within the province of this court to decide the point, I should hold that there is not now, and never has been, a case of plague in this city."

The local board of health that discovered the plague was removed, as was the State board of health that confirmed the prevalence of the disease. The governor of the State sent a remarkable message to the Legislature in which he denounced those who said plague existed in San Francisco, and appointed a committee of physicians and big business men to go to the California metropolis and make an "impartial" investigation. The business men on the committee included the biggest bankers and merchants in California. They reported in the most positive terms that there was no plague.

Dr. Kinyoun, the Marine Hospital Surgeon in charge, held his ground. Dr. Kinyoun was shortly transferred to Detroit. His successor said there was plague. His successor was shortly transferred to a distant city.

Of course, no one now denies that black plague was in San Francisco precisely when Dr. Kinyoun said it was. Even the eminent bankers and merchants who certified that it wasn't there admit that they were in "error." It is nowhere denied that there were more than 200 cases. It is nowhere denied that there were more than 100 deaths.

Such is the situation that has been imposed upon us by a system that places private profits above human life. Having painfully accumulated the knowledge with which we could combat the great disease, we are unable to apply it because we do not own and therefore cannot manage our own country.

"We look with horror on the black plague of the Middle Ages," said Professor Norton. "The black plague was but a passing cloud, compared with the white plague visitation."

CHAPTER XI
IF NOT SOCIALISM—WHAT?

I have never seen you, but I know you. Your knuckles are bloody from continued knocking at the door of happiness. The harder you knock, the bloodier your knuckles become. But the door does not open. It stands like an iron gate between you and the desires of your soul.

What is the matter with this world? Was it made wrong? Is it a barren spot to which too many have been sent? After Mr. Rockefeller and Mr. Morgan had been sent, should you have been kept? Is this their world and are you an intruder here?

You are not an intruder here. You know that. You have as good a right here as anyone else. But perhaps, nevertheless, this world was made wrong? If you had the power to make worlds, could you make a better one? Could you make fairer skies? Could you make greener fields? Could you improve the sun? Could you make better people?

Perhaps you could do none of these things? If not, what is the matter with this world? Look at it again. Here it is—spinning beneath your feet as it has spun since the dawn of time, and, never before, since the dawn of time, has it been such a world as it is now. Never before, since the dawn of time, was it so well suited to your purposes as it is now.

Your ancestors enjoyed no material thing that they had not wearily created with their hands. You need create nothing with your hands. You need but to touch with the tips of your fingers the iron hands that can make what man could never make so well. Whatever machinery can make, you can have. And, to drive this machinery, you have the forces of the sun, as they come to you in the form of steam and electricity.

Make no mistake—good, bad or indifferent as this world may be, it is at least moving. None of your ancestors ever lived in such a world. And none of your descendants will ever live in such a world as we live in to-day.

Edison once pictured to me the world that he already sees dawning. It was a wonderful world, because it was filled with wonderful machinery. Cloth would go into one end of a machine and come out at the other end finished suits of clothes, boxed and ready for the market. Every machine, instead of making a part of a thing, would make the complete thing and put it together. The world would be smothered with wealth.

But there was one disquieting feature about his world. There was not much room in it for men. Each machine, attended by but a single man, would do the work of hundreds of men. Moreover, that one man need not be skilled.

He need be but the merest automaton. Only the inventor of the machine need have brains.

Maybe Edison was dreaming. The easy way is to say he was dreaming. I, who know him, have my doubts. Edison always dreams before he does, but everything that he dreams seems pitifully small beside what he does. He dreamed of the electric light before he made it, but his dream was paltry beside the light he made. And, the dynamo of his dream was a wheelbarrow beside the dynamo that to-day sings its shrill song around the world.

This much, however, is not a dream. Some of the automatic machinery that Edison spoke of is already here. One man behind a machine is doing the work of hundreds of men. Men are becoming a drug upon the labor market. More than five millions are often out of work. As invention proceeds, the percentage of the population who cannot find work must increase.

What is going to become of these men? Do you expect them to starve quietly? Do you believe they will make no outcry? Do you believe they will raise no hand against a world that raises both hands against them? Moreover, what kind of a world is it in which the greater the machinery, the greater the curse to the men who run machinery? We do not yet live in such a world, it is true, but if Edison be not in error, we shall soon live in it? What shall we do when machinery does everything?

This may seem like a far cry, but it isn't. The germ of the Socialist philosophy is contained in this one word "machinery." Let us put the spot-light upon that word and show everything that is in it.

Suppose there were one machine in this country that was capable of producing every material thing that human beings need or desire. Suppose the machine were so wonderfully automatic that it could be perfectly operated by pushing a button, once a day, in a Wall Street office.

Beside this push-button, suppose there were another button that operated all of the railroads in the country; passenger trains automatically starting and stopping at the appointed places; freight trains automatically taking on and discharging their cargoes. Not a human being at work anywhere.

Imagine also one man owning this great machine and the railroads.

The rest of the race, if it were to remain law-abiding, would be compelled to change the law or starve to death, would it not? What else could the race do? Nobody would have any work. Nobody would therefore have anything with which to buy. The single giant machine might be capable of producing, with the push-button help of its owner, more necessities and luxuries than the entire race could consume. The automatic railway system might be capable of delivering to every door everything that everybody might want. The single owner might have more billions of dollars than Mr. Rockefeller has cents. But nobody else would have anything.

What I am trying to show is that the private ownership of machinery is a gigantic wrong. If it were not a wrong, the world would be helped by the private ownership of a single machine fitted to produce every material thing that the race needs. If the people owned such a machine, there would certainly be no more poverty. There would be no more poverty because the people would get what the machine produced.

If this be plain, let us further consider the present situation.

We live in a wonderful world.

It is big enough and rich enough to enable everybody in it to live in comfort.

But hundreds of millions throughout the world do not live in comfort because the progress of the world has brought relatively little to them.

They have no share of stock in the earth—somebody who has a little piece of paper in his hand claims the ownership of the spot of earth upon which they wish to lay their heads and charges them rent for using it.

Another little group own all of the machinery, handing out jobs here and there to the men who offer to work for the least.

Nor is this a chance situation. A small class has always robbed the great class. It has been and is the rule of the world. The methods of robbery have been changed. Method after method has been abandoned as the people awakened to the means by which they were being robbed. But robbery has never been abandoned. The small, greedy, cunning class that will not be content with what it can earn is here to-day, playing the old game with a new method.

Socialists declare the new method is to own the industrial machinery with which all other men must work. You may not agree with this. Probably you do not. If you do not, will you kindly answer some questions?

Why do a few men, who will work with no machinery, want to own all of the machinery in the country?

Would these men care to own any machinery if there were not an opportunity in such ownership to get money?

Where can the money they get come from except from the wealth that is produced by the men who work with their machinery?

So long as a few men own all of the machinery, must not all other men be at their mercy?

How can anyone get a job so long as the men who own the machinery say he can have no job?

How can anyone demand a wage that represents the full value of his product so long as the capitalist refuses to pay any wages that do not assure a profit to him?

Mr. Roosevelt and some others would have you believe that all of these wrongs can be "regulated" into rights. They would have you believe that only "strong" commissions are necessary to make all of these wrongs right. But Mr. Roosevelt and some others do not know what they are talking about. This is not a matter of opinion but a matter of fact. Men have talked as they talk since robbery began. History records no instance of one of them that made good. During all of the years that Mr. Roosevelt was in the White House, he never appointed a commission that was "strong" enough to make good.

We have it upon the authority of no less a man than Dr. Wiley that Mr. Roosevelt's commission to prevent the poisoning of food was not strong enough to make good. The food-poisoning went on.

I mention Mr. Roosevelt's food commission because it is a shining example of what his "strong" commission theory of government cannot do. Mr. Roosevelt, unquestionably, is and was opposed to the poisoning of food. He appointed a commission to stop one kind of poisoning. But, for reasons that you, as well as anyone else, can surmise, the commission decided in favor of the food-poisoners instead of in favor of the public. Which brings us to this question: If Mr. Roosevelt could not appoint a commission "strong" enough even to prevent the poisoning of food, what reason have you to believe that he or anyone else could appoint a commission strong enough to prevent capitalists from robbing workingmen?

You who oppose Socialism do so, no doubt, largely because you believe the people could not advantageously own and manage their own industrial machinery. We who advocate Socialism reply that it is much easier to manage what you own than it is to manage what someone else owns. The facts of history show that it is practically impossible to manage what someone else owns. That is what we are trying to do to-day—and we are failing at it. We are trying to manage the trusts. Fight as we will, the trusts are managing us. They fix almost every fact in our lives. They begin fixing the facts of our lives even before we are born. They determine even whether all of us shall be born. It is a well-known fact that when times are bad, the birth-rate decreases. Having the power to make bad times, the trusts also have the power to diminish the number of births. The trust panic of 1907 unquestionably prevented thousands of children from being born. No one can ever know how many, but we do know that both marriages and births decreased.

In view of such facts as these, is it not idle to talk about "regulating" the property of others? Is it not stupid to believe that in such regulation lies our greatest hope of material well-being? You must admit that, thus far, the process of regulation has gone on painfully slowly. If poverty, the fear of poverty and enforced idleness are any indications of the progress of the country, it is difficult to see that we have made any progress. Never before were so many millions of men out of work in this country as there were during the panic of 1907. Never before were so many millions of human beings so uncertain of their future. A few men hold us all in the hollows of their hands. Our destinies lie, not in ourselves, but in them.

Is it not so? Don't be blinded by "commissions," political pow-wow and nonsense—is it not so? If it is so, how much progress have we made toward getting rid of poverty by trying to regulate property that we do not own? We have been playing the game of "regulation" for more than a generation. It has done nothing for you. How many more generations do you expect to live? Are you willing to go to your grave with this pestilential question of poverty still weighing upon your heart? Are you willing to go out of the world feeling that you never really lived in it—that it was only a place where you toiled and sweat and suffered while others lived?

We Socialists put it to you as a common-sense affirmation that your time can come now if you and all others like you will join in a political effort to make it come.

Any political partisan will make you the same promise, but you know, from sad experience, that their promises are worthless. We ask you to consider whether our promises are worthless.

We promise you, for instance, that if you will give us power you need never again want for work. If the people, through the government, owned the trusts and other great industries, why should anybody ever again want for work? Thenceforward, the great plants would always be open. No factory door would ever be closed so long as there was a demand for the product of the factory. If the demand for goods were greater than the capacity of the factories, the number of factories would be increased. Nothing is simpler than to increase the number of factories. Only men and materials are required. We have an abundance of each.

But we promise you more. We promise you that, if you will give us power, we will give you not only the continuous opportunity to work, but we will give you continuous freedom from robbery. Again, nothing is simpler than to work without robbery. All that is necessary is to enable the worker to go to work without walking into anyone's clutches. No one can now go to work without walking into many men's clutches. When a man goes to work for the Steel Trust, he walks into the clutches of everybody who owns the stocks or the bonds of the trust. When a man goes to work for a railway company, he walks into the clutches of every person who owns the stocks or the bonds of the railway company. In other words, the stock and bondholders of these institutions, by virtue of their control of the machinery involved, have it in their power to say whether the worker shall work or not work. They say he shall not work unless they can make a profit upon his labor. The worker cannot haggle too long because he must labor or starve. Therefore, he comes to terms. He walks into the clutches of those who want to rob him of part of what he produces. He consents to work for a wage that represents only a part of what he has produced.

That is robbery. You may call it business, but it is robbery. If robbery is anything, it is the taking of the property of another against his will. The worker knows his wage is not all he earns. He resents the fact that he must toil long and hard for a poor living, while his employer lives in luxury without doing any useful labor. But the worker has no alternative. He must consent. He does consent.

Under Socialism, there would be no such robbery, because goods would not be produced for profit. Goods would be produced only because the people wanted them. Whatever the people wanted would be produced, not in niggardly volume, but in abundance.

Decent homes, for instance, would be produced. Millions of people in the great cities now live in houses that are death-traps. They are not houses, in the sense that country dwellers understand the word, but dingy rooms, piled one upon another in great blocks. Light seldom enters some of them. Fresh air can hardly get into any of them. The germs of tuberculosis abound. The germs of other diseases swirl through the dust of the streets. The death-rate is abnormally high—particularly the death-rate of children. Yet, nothing would be simpler, if the profit-seeking capitalists were shorn of their power, than to give every human being in this country a decent home.

The best material out of which to make a house is cement or brick. Either is better than wood because wood both rots and burns. There is practically no limit to the number of cement and brick houses that could be built in this country. Every State contains enough clay and other materials to build enough houses to supply the whole country. If the five millions of men who were out of work for many years following the panic of 1907 could have been employed at house-building, they themselves would not only have been prosperous, but the American people would have been housed as they had never been housed before. If the two millions of men who are always denied employment, even in so-called "good" times, were continuously engaged in house-building, good houses would be so numerous that we should not know what to do with them.

The same facts apply to all other necessities of life. The nation needs bread. Some are starving for it all the while. Yet what is simpler than the furnishing of bread? We know how to grow wheat. With the scientific knowledge that the government could devote to wheat growing, combined with the improved machinery that a rich government could bring to bear upon the problem, the wheat-production of the country could easily be multiplied by four. Little Holland and little Belgium, with no better soil than our own, raise almost four times as much wheat to the acre as we do. And, with wheat once grown, nothing is more simple than to make it into flour. Probably we already have enough milling machinery to make all the flour we need. If not, we could easily build four times as many mills. We should never be unable to build more mills until we had no unemployed men to set to work. And, if we had no unemployed men to set to work, we should have, for the first time in the history of the world, a completely happy nation.

Do you doubt any of these statements? How can you doubt them? We have the men. We have the materials. The only trouble is that they are kept apart. They are kept apart because a few men control things and will not allow men and material to come together unless that means a profit for the few men. We Socialists purpose to put them together. If they were put together, how much longer do you believe the people would have to shiver in winter for lack of woolen clothing? There is no secret about raising sheep. We have vast areas upon which we could raise more than we shall ever need. Even a concern like the Woolen Trust—the head of which was indicted for conspiring to "plant" dynamite at Lawrence to besmirch the strikers—even such a concern enables some of us to wear wool in the winter time. How many more do you believe would wear wool if the United States government were to take the place of this concern as a manufacturer of woolen goods? Do you believe anybody would be compelled to suffer from cold for lack of woolen clothing? How can you so believe? The government, if necessary, could build four woolen mills for every one that exists. The government could not fail to supply the people's needs. And, with all goods sold at cost, prices would be so low that the people could buy.

These, and many other possibilities, are entirely within your reach. You can realize them now. Will you kindly tell when you expect to realize them by voting for the candidates of any other party except the Socialist party? No other party except the Socialist party proposes to put men and materials together. Every other party except the Socialist party proposes that a small class of men shall continue to own all of the great industrial machinery, while the rest shall continue to be robbed as the price of its use. Every other party except the Socialist party proposes that a small body of men shall continue to graft off the rest by wringing profits from them. No party except the Socialist party puts the people above profits.

Even Mr. Roosevelt and his party do not. Mr. Roosevelt stands as firmly for the principle of profits as does Mr. Morgan. Mr. Roosevelt differs from the most besotted reactionary only in his hallucination that he could appoint "strong" commissions that would successfully regulate other people's property. Mr. Roosevelt does not seem to recognize that, so long as profits are in the capitalist system, the workers must not only be robbed of part of what they produce, but that they must be periodically denied even the right to work at any wage. Nor does he seem to realize that, if he were to reduce the profits to the point where there was not much robbery, the capitalists would no longer have any incentive for remaining in business.

With profits eliminated, or cut to the vanishing point, the capitalist system cannot stand.

With profits not eliminated or cut near the vanishing point, the people cannot stand.

Therefore, Mr. Roosevelt is trying to bring about the impossible. He is trying to prevent the people from being robbed without destroying the power of the capitalist to live by robbery. Mr. Roosevelt probably would like to decrease, somewhat, the extent to which capitalists practice robbery. But he is not willing to take away from them the power to rob.

If Mr. Roosevelt were chasing burglars instead of the Presidency, we should first laugh at him and then put a new man on the force in his place. Imagine a policeman trying to prevent burglary by "regulating" the burglars, saying to them in a hissing voice: "Now, gentlemen, this burglary must stop. We really can have no more of it. None of you must carry a 'jimmy' more than four feet long. Any burglar caught with more than twenty skeleton keys will be sent to prison."

Yet that is practically what Mr. Roosevelt says to the capitalists. The "jimmy" of the capitalist is his ownership of the tools with which his employees work, but Mr. Roosevelt makes no move to take this instrument from the men who are despoiling the workers. All that Mr. Roosevelt purposes to do is to place a limit upon the amount that the capitalist can legally abstract. And he depends upon "strong" commissions to keep the ferocious capitalist in order.

We Socialists have no faith in such measures. We frankly predict their failure, precisely as twenty years ago we predicted the failure of the Sherman Anti-Trust Law. We were then known to so few of our own people that not many persons had the pleasure of calling us fools. Now, nobody wants to call us fools for that. We are now fools because we do not believe in Wilson or in Roosevelt.

We are not content to await the verdict of time, but we await it with confidence. We dislike to waste twenty-five more years in chasing up this

Roosevelt blind alley, but if you should determine to make the trip—which we hope you will not—we shall still be on the main track when you come back.

If somebody else had the key to your house and would not let you in unless you paid him his price, you would not value highly the services of a policeman who should tell you that the way to deal with the gentleman was to "regulate" him. If the gentlemen had locked you out upon an average of four times a week, you would feel even less kindly disposed toward such a policeman.

We Socialists feel that the capitalist class has keys that belong to the American people, and that it has used and is using those keys to prevent the people from using their own, except upon the payment of tribute.

We feel that the capitalist class holds the keys to our workshops and will not let us enter except upon such tribute terms as they can wring from us.

We feel that the capitalist class has the keys to our coal fields and will not let us be warm in winter except upon the payment of money that should go, perhaps, for food or clothing.

We feel that the capitalist class has the keys of our national pantry and compels those to go hungry whom it has denied the right to work.

In short, we feel that the capitalists have the keys of our happiness—so far as happiness depends upon material things—and are compelling us to subsist upon uncertainty and fear, when security and contentment lie just at our elbows, awaiting the turn of the keys.

We Socialists are ready to stand behind any party that will pledge itself to return these keys to the people, reserving only the right to be convinced that the pledge is made in good faith and will be kept.

If Mr. Roosevelt will promise to use his best efforts to take from the capitalists the private ownership of industry, we Socialists shall believe he means business and shall begin to respect him.

If Mr. Wilson will make a similar promise, we shall feel the same toward him.

But if Mr. Roosevelt or Mr. Wilson should make such a promise, they would have absolutely no capitalist support. Mr. Perkins would not be with Mr. Roosevelt. Mr. Ryan would not be with Mr. Wilson. So far as great capitalists are concerned, Armageddon and Sea Girt would look a good deal like a baseball park two weeks after the close of the season.

All the world over, the Socialist party is the only political organization that frankly stands up to the guns and demands the keys. It is the only party that minces no words and looks for no favors from the rich. The Socialist party is avowedly and earnestly committed to the task of compelling the capitalist class to surrender the power with which it robs. And, anyone who believes that power does not lie in the private ownership of industrial machinery need only try to become rich without owning any such machinery or gambling in its products. We Socialists are willing to stake our lives on the statement that if you will transfer the ownership of industry from the capitalist class to the people, those who now constitute the capitalist class will never get another dollar that they do not work for or steal in common burglar or pickpocket fashion. If we are in error about the significance of the private ownership of industry, the transfer of such ownership to the people would not hurt the capitalist class. But the capitalist class evidently does not believe the Socialists are wrong in holding this belief, because the capitalists are fighting us tooth and nail.

Nothing is the matter with this world. Whatever is the matter is with you. You can begin to get results now if you will begin to vote right now. The election of Victor L. Berger to Congress in 1910 threw more of the fear of God into the capitalist class of this country than any other event that has happened in a generation. If fifty Socialists were in Congress, the old parties would outdo each other in offering concessions to the people.

As an illustration of what fifty Socialist Congressmen could do I will relate an incident that took place in Washington in the winter of 1912.

Berger, by playing shrewd politics, had brought about a congressional investigation of the Lawrence woolen mill strike. He had brought to Washington a carload of little tots from the mills—boys and girls—and they had spent the day telling a committee of the House of Representatives of their wrongs. The stories were heartbreaking. Here was a stunted little boy who declared he worked in a temperature of 140 degrees for $5 a week. A young girl—the daughter of a mill-worker—told of an insult offered to her by a soldier and of her own arrest when she struck him. A skilled weaver described the difficulty of keeping life in his four children on a diet of bread and molasses. Every story was different in detail, but all were alike in the depths of poverty that they revealed. The testimony bore heavily upon those who listened, and when the session was suspended for the day the members of Congress hastened quickly from the room.

As Berger walked rapidly toward the door an old man stopped him. Apparently he was a business man, 55 or 60 years old. Certainly he was not a workingman. But he had heard the day's testimony and he could not remain silent.

"Mr. Berger," he said, "I have always been against you and all Socialists. I was sorry when I heard you had been elected to Congress. But if you brought about this investigation, as I am informed you did, I want to say to you that if you were never to do another thing during your term, your election would have been more than justified. I hope your people will keep you in Congress as long as you live."

How many more men would change their minds if there were fifty Socialists in Congress? How many capitalists would change their minds as to how far they could safely go in robbing the people?

Three millions of votes for the Socialist ticket would by no means elect a Socialist president. But they would squeeze out more justice from the capitalist parties than the people have had since this government began.

Moreover, if you want the world during your own lifetime you will have to take it during your own lifetime. It will not do you much good to let your grandchildren take it during their lifetime.

APPENDIX.
NATIONAL SOCIALIST PLATFORM

(Adopted at Indianapolis, May, 1912)

The Socialist Party of the United States declares that the capitalist system has outgrown its historical function, and has become utterly incapable of meeting the problems now confronting society. We denounce this outgrown system as incompetent and corrupt and the source of unspeakable misery and suffering to the whole working class.

Under this system the industrial equipment of the nation has passed into the absolute control of a plutocracy which exacts an annual tribute of millions of dollars from the producers. Unafraid of any organized resistance, it stretches out its greedy hands over the still undeveloped resources of the nation—the land, the mines, the forests and the water-powers of every State in the Union.

In spite of the multiplication of labor-saving machines and improved methods in industry which cheapen the cost of production, the share of the producers grows ever less, and the prices of all the necessities of life steadily increase. The boasted prosperity of this nation is for the owning class alone. To the rest it means only greater hardship and misery. The high cost of living is felt in every home. Millions of wage-workers have seen the purchasing power of their wages decrease until life has become a desperate battle for mere existence.

Multitudes of unemployed walk the streets of our cities or trudge from State to State awaiting the will of the masters to move the wheels of industry.

The farmers in every State are plundered by the increasing prices exacted for tools and machinery and by extortionate rents, freight rates and storage charges.

Capitalist concentration is mercilessly crushing the class of small business men and driving its members into the ranks of propertyless wage workers. The overwhelming majority of the people of America are being forced under a yoke of bondage by this soulless industrial despotism.

It is this capitalist system that is responsible for the increasing burden of armaments, the poverty, slums, child-labor, most of the insanity, crime and prostitution, and much of the disease that afflicts mankind.

Under this system the working class is exposed to poisonous conditions, to frightful and needless perils to life and limb, is walled around with court decisions, injunctions and unjust laws, and is preyed upon incessantly for the benefit of the controlling oligarchy of wealth. Under it also, the children of the working class are doomed to ignorance, drudging toil and darkened lives.

In the face of these evils, so manifest that all thoughtful observers are appalled at them, the legislative representatives of the Republican, Democratic, and all reform parties remain the faithful servants of the oppressors. Measures designed to secure to the wage earners of this nation as humane and just treatment as is already enjoyed by the wage earners of all other civilized nations have been smothered in committee without debate, and laws ostensibly designed to bring relief to the farmers and general consumers are juggled and transformed into instruments for the exaction of further tribute. The growing unrest under oppression has driven these two old parties to the enactment of a variety of regulative measures, none of which has limited in any appreciable degree the power of the plutocracy, and some of which have been perverted into means for increasing that power. Anti-trust laws, railroad restrictions and regulations, with the prosecutions, indictments and investigations based upon such legislation, have proved to be utterly futile and ridiculous. Nor has this plutocracy been seriously restrained or even threatened by any Republican or Democratic executive. It has continued to grow in power and insolence alike under the administrations of Cleveland, McKinley, Roosevelt and Taft.

In addition to this legislative juggling and this executive connivance, the courts of America have sanctioned and strengthened the hold of this plutocracy as the Dred Scott and other decisions strengthened the slave power before the Civil War.

We declare, therefore, that the longer sufferance of these conditions is impossible, and we purpose to end them all. We declare them to be the product of the present system in which industry is carried on for private greed, instead of for the welfare of society. We declare, furthermore, that for these evils there will be and can be no remedy and no substantial relief except through Socialism, under which industry will be carried on for the common good and every worker receive the full social value of the wealth he creates.

Society is divided into warring groups and classes, based upon material interests. Fundamentally, this struggle is a conflict between the two main classes, one of which, the capitalist class, owns the means of production, and the other, the working class, must use these means of production on terms dictated by the owners.

The capitalist class, though few in numbers, absolutely controls the Government-legislative, executive and judicial. This class owns the machinery of gathering and disseminating news through its organized press. It subsidizes seats of learning—the colleges and schools—and even religious and moral agencies. It has also the added prestige which established customs give to any order of society, right or wrong.

The working class, which includes all those who are forced to work for a living, whether by hand or by brain, in shop, mine or on the soil, vastly outnumbers the capitalist class. Lacking effective organization and class solidarity, this class is unable to enforce its will. Given such class solidarity and effective organization, the workers will have the power to make all laws and control all industry in their own interest.

All political parties are the expression of economic class interests. All other parties than the Socialist Party represents one or another group of the ruling capitalist class. Their political conflicts reflect merely superficial rivalries between competing capitalist groups. However they result, these conflicts have no issue of real value to the workers. Whether the Democrats or Republicans win politically, it is the capitalist class that is victorious economically.

The Socialist Party is the political expression of the economic interests of the workers. Its defeats have been their defeats, and its victories their victories. It is a party founded on the science and laws of social development. It proposes that, since all social necessities to-day are socially produced, the means of their production shall be socially owned and democratically controlled.

In the face of the economic and political aggressions of the capitalist class the only reliance left the workers is that of their economic organizations and their political power. By the intelligent and class-conscious use of these they may resist successfully the capitalist class, break the fetters of wage slavery, and fit themselves for the future society, which is to displace the capitalist system. The Socialist Party appreciates the full significance of class organization and urges the wage earners, the working farmers and all other useful workers everywhere to organize for economic and political action, and we pledge ourselves to support the toilers of the fields as well as those in the shops, factories and mines of the nation in their struggle for economic justice.

In the defeat or victory of the working class party in this new struggle for freedom lies the defeat or triumph of the common people of all economic groups, as well as the failure or the triumph of popular government. Thus the Socialist Party is the party of the present day revolution, which marks the transition from economic individualism to Socialism, from wage slavery to free co-operation, from capitalist oligarchy to industrial democracy.

As measures calculated to strengthen the working class in its fight for the realization of its ultimate aim, the Co-operative Commonwealth, and to increase the power of resistance against capitalist oppression, we advocate and pledge ourselves and our elected officers to the following program:

Collective Ownership

1. The collective ownership and democratic management of railroads, wire and wireless telegraphs and telephones, express services, steamboat lines and all other social means of transportation and communication and of all large scale industries.

2. The immediate acquirement by the municipalities, the States or the federal government of all grain elevators, stock yards, storage warehouses and other distributing agencies, in order to reduce the present extortionate cost of living.

3. The extension of the public domain to include mines, quarries, oil wells, forests and water power.

4. The further conservation and development of natural resources for the use and benefit of all the people:

(*a*) By scientific forestation and timber protection.

(*b*) By the reclamation of arid and swamp tracts.

(*c*) By the storage of flood waters and the utilization of water power.

(*d*) By the stoppage of the present extravagant waste of the soil and of the products of mines and oil wells.

(*e*) By the development of highway and waterway systems.

5. The collective ownership of land wherever practicable, and, in cases where such ownership is impracticable, the appropriation by taxation of the annual rental value of all land held for speculation.

6. The collective ownership and democratic management of the banking and currency system.

Unemployment

The immediate government relief of the unemployed by the extension of all useful public works. All persons employed on such works to be engaged directly by the government under a workday of not more than eight hours and not less than the prevailing union wages. The government also to establish employment bureaus; to lend money to States and municipalities without interest for the purpose of carrying on public works, and to take such other measures within its power as will lessen the widespread misery of the workers caused by the misrule of the capitalist class.

Industrial Demands

The conservation of human resources, particularly of the lives and well-being of the workers and their families:

1. By shortening the workday in keeping with the increased productiveness of machinery.

2. By securing to every worker a rest period of not less than a day and a half in each week.

3. By securing a more effective inspection of workshops, factories and mines.

4. By forbidding the employment of children under 16 years of age.

5. By the co-operative organization of industries in federal penitentiaries and workshops for the benefit of convicts and their dependents.

6. By forbidding the interstate transportation of the products of child-labor, of convict labor and of all uninspected factories and mines.

7. By abolishing the profit system in government work, and substituting either the direct hire of labor or the awarding of contracts to co-operative groups of workers.

8. By establishing minimum wage scales.

9. By abolishing official charity and substituting a non-contributory system of old age pensions, a general system of insurance by the State of all its members against unemployment and invalidism and a system of compulsory insurance by employers of their workers, without cost to the latter, against industrial disease, accidents and death.

Political Demands

The absolute freedom of press, speech and assemblage.

The adoption of a gradual income tax, the increase of the rates of the present corporation tax and the extension of inheritance taxes, graduated in proportion to the value of the estate and to nearness of kin—the proceeds of these taxes to be employed in the socialization of industry.

The abolition of the monopoly ownership of patents and the substitution of collective ownership, with direct rewards to inventors by premiums or royalties.

Unrestricted and equal suffrage for men and women.

The adoption of the initiative, referendum and recall and of proportional representation, nationally as well as locally.

The abolition of the Senate and the veto power of the President.

The election of the President and the Vice President by direct vote of the people.

The abolition of the power usurped by the Supreme Court of the United States to pass upon the constitutionality of the legislation enacted by Congress. National laws to be repealed only by act of Congress or by the voters in a majority of the States.

The granting of the right of suffrage in the District of Columbia with representation in Congress and a democratic form of municipal government for purely local affairs.

The extension of democratic government to all United States territory.

The enactment of further measures for general education and particularly for vocational education in useful pursuits. The Bureau of Education to be made a department.

The enactment of further measures for the conservation of health. The creation of an independent Bureau of Health with such restrictions as will secure full liberty for all schools of practice.

The separation of the present Bureau of Labor from the Department of Commerce and Labor and its elevation to the rank of a department.

Abolition of the federal district courts and the United States Circuit Courts of Appeals. State courts to have jurisdiction in all cases arising between citizens of the several States and foreign corporations. The election of all judges for short terms.

The immediate curbing of the power of the courts to issue injunctions.

The free administration of justice.

The calling of a convention for the revision of the Constitution of the United States.

Such measures of relief as we may be able to force from capitalism are but a preparation of the workers to seize the whole powers of government in order that they may thereby lay hold of the whole system of socialized industry and thus come to their rightful inheritance.